Table of Contents

Summary

The Boys from Biloxi is a legal thriller written by John Grisham. Published in 2022, it tells the story of two men who are pitted against one another, as one runs a criminal enterprise and the other prosecutes crime as district attorney. An international best-selling author, Grisham worked as a lawyer for nearly a decade before becoming an author. His expertise informs the novel's descriptions of legal processes and its thematic exploration of legality versus morality.

This study guide refers to the 2022 Doubleday hardcover edition of the novel.

Content Warning: *The Boys from Biloxi* and this study guide touch on emotionally challenging and possibly triggering topics, including violence (murder, assault, statutory rape, rape), sex work, gambling, and capital punishment.

Plot Summary

The Boys from Biloxi is primarily told by an omniscient third-person narrator and has four parts: "The Boys," "The Crusader," "The Prisoners," and "The Row." It tells the story of two immigrant families, both from Croatia, that settled along Mississippi's Gulf Coast: the Malco family (originally Malokovic) and the Rudy family (originally Rudic). The families settle in Biloxi, a known hot spot for crime, including illegal alcohol (during prohibition), gambling, and sex work. The "boys" of the title are Hugh Malco and Keith Rudy, sons of Lance Malco and Jesse Rudy, respectively.

"The Boys" follows Hugh and Keith growing up together, attending the same school, going to the same church, and playing in the same baseball league. In their teens, they start down different paths. Keith plans to go to law school and follow in Jesse's footsteps; Jesse is a lawyer who eventually becomes district attorney (DA) and plans to rid Biloxi of crime. Meanwhile, Hugh wants to follow in *his* father's footsteps and plans to take over the family business, a string of nightclubs and bars in the seedy area of town known as The Strip, where illegal gambling and sex work run rampant.

Hugh and Keith both admire their fathers and are loyal to them. Each boy watches his father, an immigrant son, carve out a path to power and notoriety—albeit in very different realms. While Jesse is known as the "crusader," Lance is "the boss." Tension arises between Jesse and Lance when Jesse, as the DA, starts prosecuting club owners like Lance. Jesse starts by going after one of Lance's competitors, Ginger Redfield. He successfully manages to close Ginger's club and even brings a case against Ginger for knowingly running a bar where sex work is allowed (although Ginger walks free after jury tampering results in a mistrial).

Lance knows that if Jesse can put Ginger away, any of the crime bosses—including himself—may be next. Lance enlists the help of Biloxi's corrupt Sheriff, Albert "Fats" Bowman, and Lance's main henchman, Nevin Noll, to try to throw Jesse off. For example, they orchestrate an easy sting operation against one of Lance's competitors, giving Jesse a quick "win" that they hope will satiate his appetite for fighting crime. It doesn't work; Jesse remains determined to "clean up the Coast" (61). His efforts to do so are the focus of the novel's second part of the book, "The Crusader."

As Lance fears, Jesse ultimately does take him down—with help from undercover police officers of the state police (the Biloxi law enforcement is too corrupt to rely on) and an undercover informant who works at one of Lance's bars. Even the FBI comes to Jesse's aid, given that the corruption in the Coast's police is so rampant that taking down the area's criminals without outside muscle is impossible. Fats is the ultimate example, as he's been taking payouts from Ginger, Lance, and the other crime bosses in the area for years. Fats even has a monthly dinner with Lance at a Biloxi seafood restaurant, Baricev's, in public.

Jesse must resort to morally questionable tactics to put Lance in prison. Jesse learns from the FBI that they're looking for Hugh, who was involved in a string of robberies in his early twenties. The FBI doesn't know *who* they're looking for; they have only a composite sketch of the criminal. Jesse recognizes Hugh from the sketch. Jesse shows Lance the sketch and offers him a plea deal that includes prison time—and in exchange, Jesse won't tell the FBI about Hugh. If Lance doesn't agree, Jesse will inform the FBI (and Hugh will go to prison). To protect his son, Lance takes the deal. Lance's lawyer points out that Jesse's "ruthless" actions amount to extortion, flagging how a "good guy" like Jesse isn't *all* good.

While Lance is in prison, Hugh takes over his father's criminal activities. Hugh, angry at Jesse for locking his dad away, pays a hitman to make a mail bomb and drop it off at Jesse's office. Jesse dies immediately. Keith is then sworn in as DA and takes over for his father; his main aim is to catch the Malcos, whom he correctly assumes are responsible for Jesse's death. With the FBI's help, the people responsible for Jesse's death—Hugh, Nevin, and the bomb maker—are captured. Their capture is the focus of the third part of the book, "The Prisoners." Nevin and the bomb maker cut deals with the prosecution and turn on Hugh, testifying against him. For orchestrating the hit, Hugh is convicted of capital murder and is sentenced to death.

The book's final part, "The Row," returns the focus to "the boys," Hugh and Keith. While Keith rises through the ranks of politics, graduating from DA to Attorney General (AG), Hugh awaits execution on death row. His lawyers appeal his conviction multiple times. Hugh's final effort to avoid the death penalty occurs when he petitions the governor of Mississippi for clemency. However, the governor—now a connection of Keith's—consults Keith about whether to issue clemency. Keith tells the governor, "I want him [Hugh] executed" (445), sealing Hugh's fate. On the night of Hugh's execution, Keith visits him in prison, and the men talk. Hugh tells Keith that the bomb wasn't meant to kill Jesse; Keith believes him. Hugh has accepted his fate and shows Keith no ill will. Keith doesn't stay to watch the execution. As he leaves, Hugh tells him: "So long, pal. I'll see you on the other side" (454).

Background

Authorial Context: John Grisham

Grisham practiced law for almost 10 years before becoming a full-time author. His books are predominantly legal thrillers that reflect his expertise, and he's a two-time winner of the Harper Lee Prize for Legal Fiction. Although no longer a practicing lawyer, Grisham remains active in law-related causes: For example, he serves on the board of directors of the Innocence Project and Centurion Ministries, two organizations that work to exonerate people who are wrongfully convicted of crimes.

The Boys from Biloxi, like many of Grisham's works, benefits from the author's personal experience in and in-depth knowledge of the US criminal justice system. Broadly, this informs the book's intricate plot details on processes such as arraignment, trial, and appeals procedures. In addition, Grisham demonstrates familiarity with specific laws, such as the "nuisance law" that the character Jesse uses to lock away key criminals. Grisham takes care to explain these proceedings and the relevant laws, aware that his audience may not share his knowledge.

Many of Grisham's works focus on the complexities and deep-rooted problems of the US criminal justice system, such as people being wrongfully convicted of crimes. His criticism of the criminal justice system is evident in *The Boys from Biloxi*. The narrative flags the corruption within the system that often results in guilty men walking free and innocent men being locked away. The character Sheriff "Fats" Albert Bowman is the prime example (although, in the narrative, Fats eventually does come to justice—but only after many years of blatantly flouting the law).

Additionally, Grisham raises the curtain on the complexities of incarceration as a whole. The narrative includes depictions of what happens inside prisons, including gang wars and violence among criminals. It even asserts that death row is the safest place for prisoners —because it holds them in solitude so that they have no contact with other criminals. The narrative also hints at the difficulties of rehabilitation —for instance, in the difficulties that Lance faces after he's freed from prison; his wife has left him, his son is on death row, and his crime empire has crumbled.

Grisham is a vocal opponent of the death penalty and hints at this viewpoint in *The Boys from Biloxi*. Hugh ends up on death row and, despite many appeals and a final request for clemency, is executed. Grisham's criticism of the death penalty is apparent in the execution of another inmate: The procedure is botched, resulting in a drawn-out and painful process. Although the book doesn't fully assert a stance on whether capital punishment is "right" or "wrong," the author makes a clear choice to emphasize (in grotesque detail) how inhumane an execution can be if botched. Grisham's authorial lens shatters any misconception that executions are like "peacefully falling asleep."

Chapter Summaries & Analyses

Part 1, Chapters 1-6

Part 1: "The Boys"

Part 1, Chapter 1 Summary

The book opens with an overview of Biloxi's history, presented by the omniscient third-person narrator. Biloxi started as a resort and fishing community on the Gulf Coast and later developed a thriving underworld of illegal alcohol (during the prohibition area), drugs, gambling, and sex work: "The biggest obstacle facing any attempts at reform was the longtime corruption of the police and elected officials" (5). A "Dixie Mafia" developed, "a loose assortment of bad boys and misfits who preferred crime over honest work" (6). Although they had no central group or leader, over time one club owner consolidated his holdings and gained influence; he became known as "the boss." The narrative later reveals that "the boss" is Lance Malco, father of Hugh Malco—one of the "boys" referred to in the title.

Part 1, Chapter 2 Summary

The narrative introduces the two "boys from Biloxi," Keith Rudy and Hugh Malco, both born in 1948, one month apart. Both grow up in Biloxi, attend the same school, go to the same Catholic church, and play baseball together. As kids, they're friends; the book follows their progression to enemies, as Hugh follows in his father's footsteps (a club owner/"the boss") to pursue a life of crime, and Keith follows in *his* father's footsteps (a lawyer/District Attorney) to clean up Biloxi crime.

Part 1, Chapter 3 Summary

This chapter describes Hugh's family history, starting with his grandfather, Oran Malokovic, who came from Croatia to New Orleans in 1912. In the US, Oran's name became "Aaron Malco." Lance is one of Aaron's sons. Lance fights in World War II and, in 1947, marries Carmen

Coscia, who then gives birth to Hugh. Lance starts investing in illegal businesses, like a casino/bar with waitresses that also work as sex workers. Lance later opens a second, similar club, called Red Velvet. These seedy clubs help shape "The Strip," a part of Biloxi where unlicensed gambling, sex work, and other illegal activities take place.

Part 1, Chapter 4 Summary

Keith's family history is similar to Hugh's. Likewise, Keith's grandfather immigrated from Croatia to New Orleans in the early 1900s. His original name was "Rudic," but this became "Rudy" in the US. Keith's father, Jesse Rudy, was born in 1924. Like Lance, Jesse also fought in World War II. After the War, Jesse married a girl named Agnes. He took advantage of the GI bill to go to college and became Biloxi's first local lawyer of Croatian descent: "Jesse Rudy's success became the source of many proud stories on the Point" (28). Jesse and Agnes have four children: Keith, Beverley, Laura, and Timothy.

Part 1, Chapter 5 Summary

A description of the rise of criminal activity in Biloxi opens with the words: "The price war began in a brothel" (30). A gangster named Cleveland buys a club on The Strip called Foxy's and starts offering sex workers at cheaper rates: "While there was no set price for a half an hour of pleasure with a girl, the generally accepted rate, and one tacitly agreed upon by the owners, was twenty dollars" (30). As a result, other clubs lose business. Lance sends his main henchman, Nevin, to beat up Cleveland—who ends up in the hospital in a coma. "The price war was over" (35). Foxy's is shut down, and Lance buys the property. "With four clubs now under this thumb, Lance Malco controlled the largest share of vice along the Coast" (36).

Part 1, Chapter 6 Summary

Hugh slowly enters Lance's criminal world. After an injury, his interest in baseball wanes. At 16, he starts hanging around Lance's clubs and starts sleeping with one of the club's sex workers, "Cindy," who's only 15. When a customer physically assaults Cindy, Hugh joins Nevin to visit the assailant. Nevin beats the man up while Hugh watches. Although the man calls the police, they don't take any action against Nevin because they know he works for Lance (who is paying off Biloxi law enforcement).

Part 1, Chapters 1-6 Analysis

The book's first chapters provide detailed context and set the stage for the action to come (culminating in a courtroom trial that pits the Rudys against the Malcos). The historical context about Biloxi serves to demonstrate how deeply crime is ingrained in the community. Illegal activities date as far back as the 1920s prohibition era, when Biloxi was known for serving alcohol: "The biggest obstacle facing any attempts at reform was the longtime corruption of the police and elected officials" (5).

Eventually, Jesse takes on the role of "reformer," in Part 2 of the book (entitled "The Crusader"). However, Part 1, "The Boys," focuses on the two polarizing characters of the narrative: Hugh and Keith, childhood friends who later become enemies. To explicate this "friends-to-enemies" story arc, the book starts by examining the boys' similarities. They're both born the same year, in Biloxi, to immigrant families of Croatian descent:

> Their families lived two streets apart. Their parents and grandparents knew each other well. They went to the same Catholic church, the same schools, played in the same streets, sandlots, and beaches, and fished with their fathers in the Gulf on lazy weekends (8).

One of the strongest bonds between Keith and Hugh is the all-American game of baseball; both are above-average players as kids. The author's choice to have two kids from immigrant families play baseball exemplifies how families from other countries adapt "traditional" American pastimes and integrate into the United States. In the cases of Keith's and Hugh's families, even their family names are adapted: "Malokovic" becomes "Malco," and "Rudic" becomes "Rudy." This immigrant background is another similarity and bond between the two boys, who ultimately grow up to become enemies.

The impetus for the schism between Keith and Hugh starts with their families. While Hugh follows in his father's footsteps to pursue a life of crime, Keith follows in *his* father's footsteps to try to rid Biloxi of crime. This introduces the theme of **Familial Identity and Legacy**, which the narrative explores further in later chapters. Although Keith and Hugh are childhood friends, their loyalties ultimately lie with their respective families—specifically their fathers.

Grisham sets up this story arc by highlighting the differing paths of Lance and Jesse; the fathers' paths that ultimately shape their sons' paths. Much like Hugh and Keith, Lance and Jesse share many traits: Both are immigrant sons from Croatia, grew up in Biloxi, served in World War II, and got married shortly after. However, while Jesse goes to law school and becomes a lawyer, Lance gets into business and started opening clubs, bars, and casinos. Jesse is the immigrant kid who "made good," known as the first local lawyer of Croatian descent in the area: "Jesse Rudy's success became the source of many proud stories on the Point" (28). Meanwhile, Lance establishes a reputation as a savvy businessman —albeit with a dark side: "With four clubs now under this thumb, Lance Malco controlled the largest share of vice along the Coast" (36).

In addition, the book's early chapters demonstrate the brutality of the criminal underworld that Lance helps shape. For example, when Mr. Cleveland, the owner of Foxy's club, starts a "brothel" price war, Lance reacts by sending Nevin to assault him. Mr. Cleveland ends up in the hospital and closes down Foxy's. The narrative also reveals how Hugh is exposed to this world of violence as a young man. When he's a teenager, he accompanies Nevin on a mission to beat up a man who assaulted Cindy, a sex worker in one of Lance's clubs. Nevin's attack on the man is described in graphic detail. Hugh observes the incident and seems inspired by it, taking up boxing shortly after. The narrative establishes that Hugh may be a teenager but is already sliding into the violent underworld.

Part 1, Chapters 7-13

Part 1: "The Boys"

Part 1, Chapter 7 Summary

This chapter reveals the relationship between Lance and Biloxi's corrupt law enforcement. Every month, Lance and Nevin meet with Sheriff Albert "Fats" Bowman and his deputy, Rudd Kilgore, at a seafood restaurant, Baricev's, to exchange information. When an out-of-towner, Ginger Redfield, opens a new bar on The Strip, Fats and Rudd investigate—and give Lance information. Fats and Rudd also visit Ginger and tell her that she owes them $1,000 a month for "protection," revealing how they profit from the club owners and crime bosses.

Part 1, Chapter 8 Summary

Jesse's rising legal career is on the rise. He starts working as an associate in a local law firm and establishes a reputation for being an upstanding, moral man and lawyer. Some concerned locals in Biloxi approach Jesse about running for district attorney. They believe that he could be the aggressive DA they need to "clean up the Coast" (61). Driving this desire for change is a new vice that's entered Biloxi—drugs. Jesse is reluctant: "Jesse had no interest in jeopardizing the safety of his family [...] But once planted, the idea would not go away" (62)

Part 1, Chapter 9 Summary

As a teenager, Hugh continues to descend into the underworld of Lance's businesses. He quits baseball and takes up boxing. One of his most famous fights is against a boy named "Fuzz" Foster. Lance is proud of Hugh's burgeoning boxing career. Keith and Hugh are still friends, and Keith goes to Hugh's matches to cheer him on.

Part 1, Chapter 10 Summary

Lance is cheated out of money in a shady business deal with a man named Marcus Dean Poppy. Marcus and his henchman Earl Fortier purport to sell Lance a club owned by Marcus, the Carousel Lounge. Marcus and Earl take Lance's money and then claim that the Carousel Lounge has been raided by the IRS—and is temporarily closed. Then, Marcus and Earl sell the Carousel Lounge to one of Lance's competitors, Ginger. In revenge, Nevin shoots Earl and his girlfriend Rita; Fortier dies, but Rita survives and identifies Nevin as the killer. Nevin then tracks down Marcus and threatens to kill him as well—unless he returns Lance's money. Marcus pays Nevin and flees to Texas.

Part 1, Chapter 11 Summary

On trial for Earl's murder, Nevin engages criminal defense lawyer Joshua Burch (whom Lance pays) to counter the young public prosecutor, Pat Graebel. It seems like an open-and-shut case because Rita survived the shooting and identified Nevin as the shooter. However, with Lance's money and influence, the case falls apart. Rita is paid off to leave town and doesn't testify. Rita's neighbor, who previously claimed he saw Nevin flee the crime scene, is likewise paid off and leaves town. Meanwhile, sex workers from Lance's clubs—claiming to be simple waitresses to win over the jury—provide Nevin with an alibi: "Poor young Pat Graebel stood at the podium, the butt of the joke, the fool of the hour, the hotshot prosecutor whose case had vanished into thin air" (93). The jury returns a "not guilty" verdict.

Part 1, Chapter 12 Summary

Keith and Hugh, who are still in high school—and still friends—enjoy an innocent summer of fun. Keith, Hugh, and two of their friends, Joey Grasich and Denny Smith, are all 16 years old. They spend a weekend boating, chasing girls, and attending illegal cock fights (which they gain access to through Hugh's connection to Nevin). Lance is aware of Hugh's small indiscretions, like watching illegal cockfights, but doesn't care: "Hugh was only sixteen but was mature for his age and could certainly take care of himself. He was showing no interest in college and that was fine with Lance as well. The boy was needed in the family business" (102).

Part 1, Chapter 13 Summary

It's 1966. Marcus Dean Poppy is found dead in New Orleans, and the news reaches Biloxi: "Those who read the story and knew the players in Biloxi's underworld figured Lance Malco had finally settled another old debt" (103). Meanwhile, the Carousel Lounge, which Marcus sold to Ginger, has gained popularity—and Ginger has acquired other businesses on The Strip as well: "A showdown was looming. Tension was in the air as both gangs watched each other. Fats Bowman knew the streets and had cautioned both crime lords against outright warfare" (104). The sheriff's interests are purely selfish, as violence like shootings would result in the state police or even federal agents getting involved—and thus Fats wouldn't be able to collect his usual payouts from the gangs.

Meanwhile, Jesse has decided to run for DA. He tells his family when Keith is home from college for Christmas break. Keith "was proud of his parents for the decision and he couldn't wait to start campaigning" (105). During the same visit home from college, Keith meets "the old gang" (Hugh, Denny, Joey) to catch up. Hugh is no longer boxing and is focusing on his father's businesses, working in his clubs. Keith doesn't tell his friends about Jesse's plans to run for DA: "[Keith] acted as though all was well, but he knew that these moments were fleeting. The friendships were about to change, or vanish altogether [...] For him and Hugh, it was probably their last beer together" (108).

Part 1, Chapters 7-13 Analysis

The remainder of Part 1 continues to set the stage for the dramatic showdown between the Rudy and Malco clans. While Lance is establishing himself as the area's senior crime boss, Jesse's legal career is on the rise. He's even approached to run as Biloxi's DA to "clean up the Coast" (61). The book defines the arrival of the drug trade in Biloxi as the inciting incident for this perceived need to finally get a handle on the area's crime: "The old-fashioned sins had been around for decades, and though still illegal, they had become accepted in certain circles. But drugs presented a more ominous threat and had to be stopped. The future of the children was now on the line" (61).

Already, the narrative is clearly defining the "good" versus "bad" guys: Jesse, "The Crusader," emerges as anti-crime, and Lance as the "crime boss." However, Jesse doesn't take up the mantle of Crusader immediately. After the idea is first proposed to him, he doesn't jump on it, recognizing the dangers: "Jesse had no interest in jeopardizing the safety of his family" (62). By the end of Part 1, Jesse decides to pursue the role of DA, accelerating the narrative to the next step: a direct showdown between Jesse versus Lance.

These chapters underscore the depth of the challenge Jesse faces to "clean up the Coast" (61) by further illuminating the deeply ingrained nature of corruption in Biloxi—thanks to the introduction of a new character, Sheriff Albert "Fats" Bowman. Fats should enforce the laws. However, he ignores the criminal underworld and instead engages in extortion, collecting cash payments from the criminals for "protection." Fats works directly with Lance: Every month, Fats and his deputy Rudd meet with Lance and Nevin in public, at Baricev's seafood restaurant, to exchange information and tips; Fats doesn't even try to hide his criminal connections.

Nevin's trial for Earl's murder further drives home the seemingly impossible task Jesse faces. It seems like an easy case for the prosecution to win, as an eyewitness (Rita) saw the shooting and another witness (a neighbor) saw Nevin flee the scene. However, both witnesses are paid off—and the prosecution's case falls apart, leaving Nevin to walk free. The incident suggests how risky it is for Jesse to try to take on criminals like Lance from a professional standpoint (not just from a personal safety standpoint), given the prosecutor's humiliation: "Poor young Pat Graebel [the prosecutor] stood at the podium, the butt of the joke, the fool of the hour, the hotshot prosecutor whose case had vanished into thin air" (93).

The lines being drawn between Jesse and Lance are also trickling down to their sons. Hugh becomes increasingly involved in his father's business, something Lance encourages: "[Hugh] was showing no interest in college and that was fine with Lance as well. The boy was needed in the family business" (102). After graduating from high school, Hugh works at Lance's clubs. Meanwhile, Keith goes to law school and plans to follow in Jesse's footsteps. Keith supports his father's decision to run for DA. The boy's loyalty to their fathers exemplifies the book's theme of **Familial Identity and Legacy**—they remain loyal to the "family business," whether it's crime or the law.

Part 1 of *The Boys from Biloxi* began by emphasizing the similarities between Hugh and Keith, highlighting points like their immigrant backgrounds, their love of baseball, and their shared social context (the same school, church, sports teams). By the end of Part 1, however, the boys' differences are the focus. These differences are significant enough that they ultimately ruin the boys' friendship, informing the narrative's "friends-to-enemies" story arc. In Chapter 13, the final Chapter of Part 1, the boys have their last beer together. Keith, already knowing that Jesse will run for DA, is aware of the end ahead: "[Keith] acted as though all was well, but he knew that these moments were fleeting. The friendships were about to change, or vanish altogether. [...] For him and Hugh, it was probably their last beer together" (108), highlighting the theme of **The Dangers of Loyalty**.

Part 2, Chapters 14-21

Part 2: "The Crusader"

Part 2, Chapter 14 Summary

Jesse informs the current DA, Rex Dubisson, of his plans to challenge him by running for DA. Rex warns him, "There's nothing clean about politics around here, Jesse. You're being naive. It's a dirty game," to which Jesse replies, "It doesn't have to be" (114). Jesse then formally announces his candidacy in the local newspaper, the *Gulf Coast Register*. Lance is amused by the announcement but recognizes Jesse's mission to "clean up the Coast" (61) as a threat: "Once, many years ago, [Lance] had considered [Jesse] a friend. Those days were long gone. The new battle lines were clear and the war was on" (116). When Jesse's campaign manager discovers his tires slashed, he quits the campaign, and Keith, now 19, steps into his place.

Part 2, Chapter 15 Summary

As part of his campaign, Jesse sends out a direct mailing targeting organized crime in Biloxi. Lance sees it as a threat and "the first sign of open warfare from Jesse Rudy" (123). As a countermeasure, Lance's supporters send out a mailing featuring a photo of a woman who claims to have been raped by Jarvis Decker—a criminal Jesse defended in a domestic abuse case. The mailing claims that Jesse "cozies up" to violent criminals (125). A judge ultimately puts a stop to the dirty campaigning tactic of slanderous direct mailings, but the damage has already been done to Jesse's campaign. Rex Dubisson wins reelection.

Part 2, Chapter 16 Summary

Lance faces a new competitor in The Strip's nightclub and vice business, Dusty Cromwell. Lance pays someone to burn down Dusty's bar. Then, the arsonist who presumably handled the job is killed—and the person who kills him sends his ear to Lance. Dusty and Lance continue to trade acts of violence. The gang war ends when a hitman, known as "the Rifleman," kills Dusty while he's walking on the beach with his girlfriend (136). The violence associated with the "gangland warfare" is now too blatant to ignore, and the *Gulf Coast Register* starts publishing articles about it. Fats assures the people that his men are investigating, but everyone knows that he's complicit. This is good news for Jesse: "More violence would only help Jesse's case. People were upset and wanted something done" (137).

Part 2, Chapter 17 Summary

Hurricane Camille batters the Florida Panhandle, causing damage to Biloxi. The storm wreaks havoc on the community, and people can focus only on necessities like shelter, food, and water. Gangsters like Lance quickly get back on their feet by getting friendly with the insurance adjusters who assess damages after the storm. Lance races to be the first person to reopen his club: "The time was right to spend big and establish a monopoly" (142).

Part 2, Chapter 18 Summary

Following Hurricane Camille, many people struggle to get insurance payouts for the damages to their homes and businesses. The main issue is that insurance policies written in Mississippi cover damage caused by wind but not water. Jesse, seeing an opportunity, opens up The Rudy Law Firm and starts representing people who want to sue the insurers. To keep up with the demand, Jesse hires lawyers Gene and Gage Pettigrew (brothers). With their help, Jesse positions himself as the "good-guy" lawyer taking on the bad insurance companies, as "[t]here was a feeling of outright hatred for the insurance companies" (147) in Biloxi.

Part 2, Chapter 19 Summary

Jesse starts taking the many lawsuits against the insurance companies to court. Judge Oliphant, who is sympathetic to the locals, presides. With Judge Oliphant's support, Jesse pushes through multiple cases and wins, which helps bolster his growing reputation as a defender of good, everyday people.

Part 2, Chapter 20 Summary

In Jesse's continuing crusade against the insurance companies, although he's winning cases, the insurance companies have yet to pay—and they find ways to delay by filing appeals. Some cases go all the way to the State Supreme Court. Meanwhile, Keith graduates from the University of Southern Mississippi at age 22. In the summer after graduating, Keith helps around Jesse's law firm. Before he leaves for law school, he meets his old school pals Joey and Denny for a drink. They tell him that they're no longer hanging out with Hugh and warn him that Hugh is trouble: "He's a total thug, Keith. You don't want to be around him" (169). Hugh has slipped into the criminal underworld: "Career gangsters like Lance Malco went to prison, or took a bullet, or they died in prison. That was Hugh's future too" (170).

Part 2, Chapter 21 Summary

The insurance companies finally settle the Hurricane Camille cases that Jesse has been representing. They agree to pay the insurance claims plus interest and living expenses. While the insurance companies still delay sending out checks until the last minute, they ultimately pay the money they're supposed to. Meanwhile, Lance and the other nightclub owners have been rebuilding: "Vice was perhaps the first industry to fully recover after the storm" (175).

Part 2, Chapters 14-21 Analysis

Part 2 shifts the focus from the boys to Jesse, following his attempts to become DA of Biloxi. Jesse's initial unsuccessful campaign for DA proves just how deeply ingrained the corruption in Biloxi is, speaking to how corruption is often driven by greed (as exemplified by Fats, who ignores crime in exchange for payment from gangs). Not only criminals are corrupt in *The Boys from Biloxi*. Politicians and everyday people are prone to temptations, like money, and thus prone to corruption.

Even Jesse himself later takes a corrupt path, resorting to extortion in his efforts to put Lance in prison. The narrative foreshadows this ironic twist —the good-guy crusader getting his hands dirty—when Rex tells Jesse, "There's nothing clean about politics around here, Jesse. You're being naive. It's a dirty game," and Jesse replies, "It doesn't have to be" (114). Jesse may believe this now, but he inevitably enters the "dirty game" and proves just as ruthless as the rest of the people involved.

The first hints at Jesse's willingness to play dirty are evident in his initial DA campaign. When he is affected by a smear campaign executed via direct mailings, Jesse responds in kind and sends out a direct mailing to Biloxi citizens calling out Lance and the other club owners' corruption. This marks a turning point in the relationship between Jesse and Lance: "Once, many years ago, [Lance] had considered [Jesse] a friend. Those days were long gone. The new battle lines were clear and the war was on" (116).

In addition, these chapters highlight the increasing danger that Jesse's mission to "clean up the Coast" (61) puts him in, foreshadowing his demise—he's killed in a hit orchestrated by Hugh. The first hint of this violence comes when his campaign manager's tires are slashed—which scares the campaign manager enough that he quits. Keith's desire to take the campaign manager's place, despite the risks, speaks to his love for and loyalty to his father, emphasizing the book's theme of **Familial Identity and Legacy**.

The Hurricane Camille storyline emphasizes how corruption negatively impacts everyday society. While everyday people are unable to get payouts from the corrupt insurers because of legal technicalities (the question of wind versus water damage), criminals like Lance use their ill-gained resources, connections, and cash to recover quickly—and even profit from the incident. Lance sees the opportunity, thinking "The time was right to spend big and establish a monopoly" (142). The narrative later notes that "vice was perhaps the first industry to fully recover after the storm" (175).

Meanwhile, Jesse sees an opportunity of his own in Hurricane Camille's aftermath: By representing the many people negatively impacted by the insurance companies' unwillingness to settle claims, Jesse bolsters his "good guy" reputation and gains support for a future DA campaign. Although Lance and Jesse are on opposite sides—bad versus good—both benefit from the hurricane that wreaks havoc on the coast. The narrative thus disputes the childish concept of good and evil, like one might find in a fairytale. In the real world, it's not that simple or "black-and-white"; there are a lot of gray areas. Jesse does upstanding work as a lawyer but still recognizes the benefits for himself personally and uses the situation to his advantage, revealing a self-serving element to his character: He's not a saintly, selfless hero. The narrative underscores this fact later when he turns to extortion to help put Lance in prison.

Although these chapters focus largely on Jesse, "The Crusader," and his rise upward in the ranks, they mention Hugh and Keith, who are the story's ultimate focus. Keith has graduated from the University of Southern Mississippi. Meanwhile, Hugh has slipped into the criminal underworld, as confirmed by character dialogue between Denny, Joey, and Keith, when Denny and Joey tell Keith that "[Hugh's] a total thug" (169). This same chapter concludes with a shocking direct statement that foreshadows what lies ahead for Hugh: "Career gangsters like Lance Malco went to prison, or took a bullet, or they died in prison. That was Hugh's future too" (170). This blatant prediction about both Lance and Hugh might break the book's narrative tension; however, the author doesn't reveal details about Hugh's future, leaving it open-ended whether Hugh will die in gang violence or die in prison (or simply rot away there).

Part 2, Chapters 22-27

Part 2: "The Crusader"

Part 2, Chapter 22 Summary

Hugh, 22, is bored of the work he does for Lance and Nevin. He meets a guy named Jimmie Crane, who convinces him to get into the weapons business. However, they need at least $10,000 to get started. To get the money, Jimmie and Hugh—with the help of a "stripper" named Sissy—start robbing small-town jewelry stores and pawn shops throughout the South. One job goes wrong, and the shop owner shoots Jimmie and Sissy dead. Hugh flees the scene and gets a job on a freighter bound for Europe; he stays away from Biloxi for six months. The FBI eventually comes through Biloxi with composite sketches of Jimmie, Sissy, and Hugh: The agents ask Fats if he knows any of the people depicted. Fats recognizes Hugh from one of the sketches but says nothing (out of loyalty to Lance).

Part 2, Chapter 23 Summary

It's 1971, an election year. Jesse decides to pursue a second run for DA and announces his candidacy. Keith supports his father's campaign. Jesse is more strategic with his campaign this time. He realizes that he'll have a better chance of winning if he can get a third candidate to go up against Rex Dubisson, splitting the votes. Jesse convinces a woman named Egan Clement to run against him, telling her that he'll appoint her as assistant DA if he wins. This time, Jesse wins the race and becomes DA; he fulfills his promise, making Egan assistant DA.

Part 2, Chapter 24 Summary

Fats and Rudd meet Lance and Nevin for their monthly dinner at Baricev's. They discuss Jesse's winning the DA race. Nevin and Lance have a plan to disarm the new DA: A new competitor of Lance's, Andy Rizzo, has opened a nightclub called Siesta that hosts illegal gambling; Nevin and Lance suggest setting up a police raid on Andy's club and supporting Jesse's subsequent prosecution. It gives Jesse an easy win and makes it look like Fats and his police will cooperate with the new DA. In fact, Fats and his men will continue conspiring with Lance. The scheme goes as planned, although Jesse is suspicious: "The case was too easy and Jesse smelled a rat" (203).

Jesse decides to go after the Biloxi "strip clubs" and bust them for illegal sex work. He finds two honest cops and has them go undercover in the clubs, wearing wires. They focus on the Carousel, one of Ginger's clubs. Once Jesse has enough proof from the undercover cops, he files a lawsuit against the Carousel, citing the state's "nuisance law," which "allowed any citizen to file suit to enjoin another citizen from pursuing activities that were illegal and detrimental to the public good" (203). Although not personally targeted, "Lance Malco was livid and realized the gravity of the assault on his businesses. If Jesse Rudy could close Carousel, any club might be next" (206). The Judge overseeing the case declares Carousel a nuisance and orders it closed; although the club is allowed to reopen following an appeal and a $10,000 bond, it's still a blow to the criminal underground.

Part 2, Chapter 25 Summary

Jesse's next step in his mission to "clean up the Coast" (61) is even bolder: He convenes a grand jury to indict Ginger personally (not the club) on four counts of promoting sex work. If convicted, Ginger could face large fines and go to jail. Lance and the other underworld criminals are rattled: Jesse is no longer going after the institutions but after the people who own them. Lance meets with Fats: "It was time to discuss what to do about Jesse Rudy" (215).

Part 2, Chapter 26 Summary

Jesse's assistant DA, Egan, starts investigating unsolved murders around Biloxi. Egan and Jesse are convinced that Lance is behind the Dusty Cromwell murder—but they can't prove it. Jesse is determined to take down Lance, one way or another. He finds a man named Haley Stofer who's in prison for running drugs; Jesse cuts a deal with Haley, helping get him out of prison early in exchange for Haley going undercover as a worker at Red Velvet or Foxy's, Lance's two main clubs. Jesse warns Haley: "These guys'll kill you in an instant. Never drop your guard" (222). Haley agrees to Jesse's terms.

Part 2, Chapter 27 Summary

The Rudy family drives to Oxford, Mississippi, to celebrate Keith's graduation from law school. While there, they meet his new girlfriend, Ainsley. After the graduation, Ginger's trial begins. The first step is jury selection. Fats and Rudd manage to obtain the jury list, and Rudd assures Lance: "Sixty names. Fats says he knows at least half of them" (224). It's apparent that Fats and Russ are planning to tamper with the jury. Although Ginger is Lance's competitor, it's in his interests that she wins her case; it would set a dangerous precedent if she lost. The trial goes ahead with a lot of public attention on it. Shortly before the jury votes, Jesse receives an anonymous note on his car that reads: "*Joe Nunzio* [one of the jurors] *got $2,000 cash to vote not guilty*" (231). Jesse ignores the note. In the end, the jury can't reach an anonymous decision, resulting in a mistrial. Ginger walks free.

Part 2, Chapters 22-27 Analysis

These chapters introduce a small subplot that at first doesn't seem significant: Hugh's spree of robberies. In the book's immediate context, this little side story about Hugh seems like it's simply adding color to the story and contributing to his characterization. However, the robberies later become a critical plot point when Jesse learns about Hugh's crimes and extorts Lance with this knowledge, convincing him to take a deal and go to prison to protect Hugh. This pivotal moment leads to Lance's imprisonment and Jesse's subsequent murder (as revenge). Thematically, Jesse's act of extortion will illustrate the inescapability of corruption, as the "good guy" gets his hands dirty by resorting to crime to get what he wants: Lance behind bars.

Jesse's actions in the DA race lay the groundwork for the revelation that he isn't totally pure. After losing the first race, Jesse is aware that he can't win by playing clean. This time, he helps take votes away from his opponent, Rex, by convincing another person, Egan, to run—and promising to make her assistant DA if he wins. It's not technically illegal but certainly unethical and undermines the idea of a fair election. Already, it's clear how Jesse has changed from his first DA race, when Rex warned him about the dirtiness of local politics and Jesse indicated his intent to stay clean. Jesse now knows that playing dirty is sometimes necessary.

Jesse's increasingly ruthless nature makes him more of a threat to Lance and the other criminals in Biloxi. The case that Jesse makes against Ginger and the Carousel is a prime example. Lance sees Jesse's going after not only the club but also the person in charge of it as a threat and meets with Fats "to discuss what to do about Jesse Rudy" (215). This ominous phrasing foreshadows the violence that Jesse will face and the increasingly risky nature of his endeavor to "clean up the Coast" (61).

Ginger's trial thus helps to elevate the tension and draw out the narrative. Theoretically, the author could have left out the entire story about Ginger and simply had Jesse go after Lance immediately. However, by using Ginger's case as an example, the author builds up to the climax —Lance's trial—more slowly, elevating the tension. The omniscient third-person narrative reveals that Jesse ultimately wants to go after Lance. However, by showing Jesse slowly moving in on his target rather than pouncing on Lance immediately, the narrative builds suspense.

Additionally, Ginger's trial explicates some of the legal points behind the action. Legal thrillers like Grisham's can't assume that the reader understands criminal code and the law. Ginger's trial allows the narrative to sprinkle explanations throughout. For example, the author explains the "nuisance law," which Jesse uses to shut down the Carousel, as a law that "allowed any citizen to file suit to enjoin another citizen from pursuing activities that were illegal and detrimental to the public good" (203).

Through Ginger's trial, the author also includes some explanation about jury selection and jury tampering. If the jury can't come to a unanimous decision, the result is a mistrial, which allows Ginger to walk free. It thus becomes apparent why jury tampering, as exemplified by juror Joe Nunzio's receiving "*$2,000 cash to vote not guilty*" (231), is such an egregious crime—just one person going astray can derail a case. These legal details again become relevant when Lance goes on trial. By that time, the narrative has provided the basic legal knowledge to follow the trial's main action points. This allows for a smoother narrative flow during Lance's trial—and a more exciting climax.

Part 2, Chapters 28-34

Part 2: "The Crusader"

Part 2, Chapter 28 Summary

After Ginger's mistrial, Lance and the other criminals on The Strip relax: "The mistrial calmed The Strip like a gin martini" (235). However, Jesse's mission isn't finished. His undercover man, Haley, is working his way up at Red Velvet. Meanwhile, Jesse meets with Judge Oliphant and reveals his suspicions that the jury was tampered with in Ginger's trial. The Judge does some investigating and confirms Jesse's suspicions: Three jury members—Joe Nunzio, Paul Dewey, and Chick Hutchinson—were bought off.

Part 2, Chapter 29 Summary

It's December 1973. Jesse reflects on the work he's done so far as DA: "Jesse's first term was almost over and he considered it unsuccessful" (242). He realizes that he needs outside help beyond Biloxi. Jesse and Keith manage to secure a meeting with the governor, a former prosecutor named Bill Waller. Governor Waller is aware of Biloxi's criminal world and even knows that Fats is complicit with the criminal activity, telling Keith and Jesse, "Fats Bowman belongs in prison" (244). Governor Waller asks Jesse how he can help him in his mission to "clean up the Coast" (61). Jesse requests the support of the state police. The Governor agrees.

Part 2, Chapter 30 Summary

In January 1974, the Mississippi Supreme Court denies the appeal in the Carousel club case—and the Carousel is closed permanently. Although it took two years, Jesse sees this as a success: "He had shuttered one of the more popular joints on The Strip, and now he could go after Ginger again. Lance Malco would be next, though he, as always, would be more complicated" (246). With the help of his undercover worker, Haley, and some undercover state policemen, Jesse gets evidence of the sex work occurring at Foxy's, one of Lance's clubs. He then convenes a grand jury to indict Lance: "By unanimous agreement, the grand jury indicted Lance Malco on one count of operation a 'place' used for prostitution and thirteen counts of causing and encouraging women to engage in prostitution" (250). Three of Foxy's managers are also indicted, and 13 women who work at Foxy's are indicted on felony charges for sex work. Lance, the managers, and the women are arrested. Meanwhile, Keith contacts the *Gulf Coast Register* and alerts them to the news. Fats, worried, flees to Florida. Jesse, his law firm's employees, and his family start getting threatening phone calls.

Part 2, Chapter 31 Summary

Foxy's is temporarily closed, and Lance's lawyer, Joshua Burch, tries various legal maneuvers to get it reopened. Similar to Ginger's case, Lance's case will hinge largely on jury selection: "The jury would be the key, as always, and the defense only needed one vote" (254). (The jury must unanimously find Lance guilty, so all it takes is one person to find him not guilty to result in a hung jury and a mistrial—just as in Ginger's case.) Hugh, 26, is "worried about his father and angry that Jesse had actually indicted Lance. He could not comprehend his dad going to prison, though he had gradually accepted the possibility" (255-56). Nevertheless, Jesse's case against Lance isn't a sure shot. He becomes worried when Haley—whose testimony helped in the indictment—runs off, scared by Nevin. Haley tells Jesse, "I got a tip from a guy at work, said he overheard Nevin Noll cussing me, calling me a snitch" (257). Haley agrees to go to Chicago, a big city where it's easier to hide out, until Lance's trial, when he'll return to testify.

Part 2, Chapter 32 Summary

Lance's defense attorney, Joshua, is watching his case fall apart. Joshua initially planned to defend Lance, the managers, and the 13 women together. However, the women and the managers start turning to other lawyers, who help them secure deals with the DA—in exchange for turning on Lance. Meanwhile, the trial date for Lance is set for March 17.

Part 2, Chapter 33 Summary

It's December. Another of Lance's ex-managers turns on him, agreeing to plead guilty and testify against Lance in exchange for a lighter sentence. To delay the trial and keep Lance out of prison, his lawyer, Joshua, wants to use health reasons. He tells Lance, "Go see Cyrus Knapp, the heart doctor. He's a quack but he'll do what I say. Tell him since you got arrested you've been having chest pains, dizziness, fatigue" (268). Lance is reluctant to "play sick" but agrees. Lance says that he isn't afraid of going to prison, and Hugh admires his dad's toughness. Lance knows he needs to start making plans for his businesses in case he must go to prison and has discussed this with Hugh: "Hugh was confident he could run the businesses in his father's absence. His father wasn't so sure" (269). Meanwhile, the narrative introduces a new character: Jackson Lewis of the FBI. Jackson meets Jesse and establishes that the FBI is ready to help him.

Part 2, Chapter 34 Summary

Joshua goes with his plans to get the trial date pushed back: "On March 3, two weeks before the trial, Burch filed a motion for a continuance, claiming Mr. Malco was too ill to defend himself. The motion included affidavits from two doctors and a pile of medical reports" (274). A new trial date is set for May 12.

Meanwhile, Jesse gets another visit from FBI agent Jackson Lewis. Jackson tells Jesse that the FBI is investigating a string of robberies along the coast—the ones that Hugh was involved in—and shows Jesse composite sketches of the three people involved. Jesse recognizes Hugh from the composite sketch and asks the FBI agent for a copy.

It's now May 5, 1975, one week before Lance's trial is set to commence. Jesse surprises the defense by (successfully) requesting that the case be tried in a neighboring county. This means that the jurors will all be selected from registered voters based in the neighboring country—not Biloxi. Jesse explains his motivation for the switch: "I'm convinced the jury in the Ginger Redfield trial was tampered with and we're not running the risk this time around" (278). The petition to have the trial moved to the neighboring county goes ahead.

Part 2, Chapters 28-34 Analysis

These chapters slowly build to what will be the book's climax: Lance's trial. Jesse quietly lays the groundwork to take down the number one crime boss: He continues to gather information from his undercover man, Haley; he has the trial location moved to another county to minimize the risk of jury tampering (as happened in Ginger's case); and he gets backing from senior law enforcement and governmental officials, like the FBI and the governor of Mississippi. Jesse's need to call in more senior officials reiterates the difficulty of his mission to "clean up the Coast" (61). This becomes even more apparent when the governor himself says, "Fats Bowman belongs in prison" (244). It's shocking that even the governor is aware of Fats's shady reputation—Biloxi isn't a big town, after all. Increasingly, it seems that many of the laws and processes meant to combat corruption, such as elections, are actually breeding grounds for corruption.

In addition, these chapters reiterate the value of Ginger's case as an authorial tool that allows the narrative to reveal relevant points about the basics of the legal process before Lance's action-packed trial. For example, Ginger's trial emphasized the danger of jury tampering and showed that unanimous agreement is needed from the jury for the trial to succeed. These chapters reiterate that fact: "The jury would be the key, as always, and the defense only needed one vote" (254). It's an interesting reminder that the jury—everyday men and women—is so pivotal in deciding criminal cases. People often joke about jury duty and wanting to get out of it, which can trivialize it. In fact, sitting on a jury is a major responsibility and can change someone's life.

The narrative also affords insights into the appeals process, reflecting on Jesse's earlier case against the Carousel. In the initial trial against the Carousel, the jury agreed with the "nuisance law" and had the club shut down. However, Gingers' lawyer appealed the decision—and, as long as the appeal was pending, the club was allowed to operate. As a result, after the initial trial, the Carousel was closed for only about a week. Now, two years later, the case has finally made its way through the appeals process: The Mississippi Supreme Court denies the appeal, and the Carousel closes permanently. It's a victory for Jesse but also demonstrates how time-consuming and tedious the legal process is. It's another "teaching moment"—something legal thrillers must do to ensure that their audience, who presumably aren't lawyers, can keep up with the legal action.

The major shock in these chapters, the highlight of the action, is Lance's indictment. The story has been building to this moment—it's the pinnacle of Jesse's mission, his ultimate goal as "The Crusader." However, by achieving this goal, Jesse puts himself in danger. Although the author hasn't yet revealed it, Jesse is later killed as a result of his pursuit of Lance. The narrative foreshadows this, reiterating the danger that Jesse faces by describing the threatening phone calls he gets after Lance's bail hearing. Additionally, the narrative hints that Hugh may be the person who brings about Jesse's death, describing his anger at his father's criminal charges: "He could not comprehend his dad going to prison, though he had gradually accepted the possibility" (255-56). The fact that Hugh fixes his mind on Jesse as the source of his father's trouble and is angry at him suggests that he may have a taste for revenge.

Underscoring the significance of Lance's indictment, Keith personally contacts the *Gulf Coast Register* to inform them of the indictment. This speaks to the importance of the media in the interplay of politics, crime, the legal system, and public opinion. The role of the media in shaping public opinion was evident previously in Jesse's DA elections, when Lance and Jesse used opposing smear campaigns to paint the other as a villain in the public eye. Here, the narrative reiterates the importance of the media in getting public opinion to shift. In this case, Jesse wants to make it clear that the "good guys" have won a victory with the indictment against Lance. It's a war not just within the courts but also within the media landscape that influences public opinion.

In the buildup to Lance's trial, these chapters further the book's argument regarding the rampant nature of corruption. Lance's lawyer, Joshua, will go to any means to help his client—even as far as falsifying medical records with the help of a shady doctor: "Go see Cyrus Knapp, the heart doctor. He's a quack but he'll do what I say. Tell him since you got arrested you've been having chest pains, dizziness, fatigue" (268). The idea works: "On March 3, two weeks before the trial, Joshua files a motion for a continuance, claiming that Mr. Malco is too ill to defend himself. The motion included affidavits from two doctors and a pile of medical reports" (274). A new trial date is set for May. Again, these details provide unique insights into the legal system. Pushing back the trial date extends the narrative as well, giving the author more time to ramp up tension, add detail to the plot, and tease out relevant subplots such as the appearance of the FBI. Through the FBI, Jesse learns of the string of robberies and realizes that Hugh is involved. When he asks the FBI for a copy of the sketch showing Hugh's face, it seems insignificant—but it later becomes a big deal when Jesse uses this sketch of Hugh to extort Lance and convince him to take a plea deal that sends him to prison; this then inspires Hugh to take out a hit on Jesse. Additionally, Jesse's plan to extort Lance signifies a moral shift, when the narrative's "hero" resorts to immoral and illegal tactics to win, throwing the entire good versus evil dichotomy into question.

Part 3, Chapters 35-42

Part 3: "The Prisoners"

Part 3, Chapter 35 Summary

Jesse meets with Joshua Burch, Lance's lawyer, to propose a plea deal. He brings the composite sketch of Hugh and tells Joshua that the FBI is looking for Hugh, adding, "I haven't said a word to the FBI yet. I can keep my mouth shut if I get the deal" (284). Joshua tells Jesse, "This is ruthless" and "It's blackmail" (284). However, he agrees to take Jesse's deal—which will involve prison time for Lance—to Lance for consideration, and Lance decides to take the deal. On May 12, Lance pleads guilty to "having control over the use of a place and knowingly allowing another person to use said place for prostitution" (287) and is sentenced to 10 years in the state penitentiary at Parchman and fined $5,000. The *Gulf Coast Register* reports the news: "MALCO PLEADS GUILTY—ORDERED TO PRISON" (287).

Part 3, Chapter 36 Summary

Keith marries his college sweetheart, Ainsley, and the entire Rudy family celebrates. The narrative then shifts to Haley, Jesse's former mole at Lance's clubs, who fled to Chicago, worried that Lance would have him killed after he testified against him. Haley is arrested for drunk driving. Haley is hoping for Jesse's help getting a lenient sentence, which had been part of the deal for testifying against Lance, but Jesse declines, telling him: "You chose to run drugs. Now you pay the price" (292). Meanwhile, Hugh is taking over his father's businesses but finding it difficult now that the FBI is lurking around Biloxi.

Part 3, Chapter 37 Summary

The man who was paid to kill Dusty Cromwell, Bayard Wolf, becomes terminally ill in February 1976. Facing the end of his life, he confesses to the murders he committed as a hitman, including that of Cromwell. Jesse has been hoping to solve the Cromwell murder for years; this is a huge breakthrough. Nevin is tipped off by a stranger:

> He told Noll that Bayard Wolf had told the cops everything before he died. They knew Malco ordered the contract and Noll handed over $20,000 to Wolf. They knew the Rifleman pulled the trigger. The Biloxi DA was investigating the Cromwell killing (302).

Part 3, Chapter 38 Summary

The narrative shifts to the perspective of a hitman—a bomb maker, Henry Taylor, who goes by "Lyle" (303). Lyle delivers a package, a bomb, to Jesse's office. Jesse takes the package into his office; it explodes, injuring numerous people in the courthouse—and killing Jesse instantly. Keith asks that Fats and his men be kept away from the crime scene, worried that they'll be involved in the cover-up. The Biloxi Chief of Police assures him that Fats and his men aren't involved; the FBI are on the scene investigating.

Part 3, Chapter 39 Summary

FBI Agent Jackson Lewis leads the investigation into Jesse's death. Meanwhile, Keith and his siblings stay with Agnes (their mother and Jesse's widow). Keith's childhood friend Joey, one of the three boys he used to hang out with in school, comes by the house to show his respects: "Seeing a childhood buddy brought out a lot of emotions, and Keith had his first long cry of the day" (313). Keith goes to the hospital to visit Egan, the assistant DA, who was injured in the blast. Henry Taylor ("Lyle"), who was injured in the blast as well (because he didn't manage to get far enough from the scene before Jesse opened the package bomb), is receiving treatment in the same hospital: "As [Keith] and [his childhood friend] Joey left [Egan's] room and headed for the elevators, they passed Room 301, semi-private. Lying in the first bed, with his leg in the air, was the man who killed Jesse Rudy" (314).

Part 3, Chapter 40 Summary

The FBI continues their investigation into Jesse's murder. Agent Lewis is suspicious of Henry Taylor ("Lyle"), who is still in the hospital and unidentified: "The man with the broken leg had not been identified, and Lewis's suspicion was growing by the hour" (316). He sets a trap for the man: The FBI will wait for him to be released from the hospital and will then follow him, hoping that he'll lead them to the person who paid him to kill Jesse. Meanwhile, Hugh and Nevin go out for a celebratory dinner: "For Hugh, the occasion was bittersweet. He was delighted Jesse Rudy was gone, but so was his father. Lance should be dining with them and savoring the moment" (316).

Part 3, Chapter 41 Summary

Jesse's murder is reported by the media, with headlines like "JESSE RUDY KILLED IN COURTHOUSE EXPLOSION," "MOB STRIKES BACK—PROSECUTOR DEAD," and "CRUSADING DA KILLED IN BILOXI" (320). The Rudy family remains in mourning. Meanwhile, Agent Lewis continues to lay the groundwork for his plan: Wait for Henry Taylor ("Lyle") to leave the hospital and follow him.

Part 3, Chapter 42 Summary

Henry Taylor ("Lyle") is released from the hospital. Unaware that the FBI is following him, he's gleefully convinced that he's gotten away with Jesse's murder and thinks to himself, "What a bunch of morons down there [in Biloxi]" (330). Keith talks to Judge Oliphant about Jesse's murder. Both are convinced that Hugh and Nevin are behind the hit, but the Judge warns Keith that proving it will likely be impossible, telling him, "Contract killings are virtually impossible because the guilty party touches nothing" (332). The chapter concludes with Jesse's funeral.

Part 3, Chapters 35-42 Analysis

Part 3 opens with a pivotal moment of character development: Jesse uses his knowledge of Hugh's involvement in the old jewelry store and pawnshop robberies to get Lance to take a guilty plea that includes prison time. It's both morally questionable and an illegal move on Jesse's part. Joshua, Lance's defense lawyer, calls Jesse out on it, saying "This is ruthless" and calling it "blackmail" (284). Jesse, who's supposed to be the morally upstanding character, is clearly willing to take immoral (and illegal) actions to get the outcome he wants: Lance in prison. The scheme works, showing how a corrupt system rewards bad behavior: Lance takes the plea and goes to prison.

In the background of the legal action these chapters focus on, the book provides brief insights into the private lives of the Rudy and Malco families. For example, Keith marries his college sweetheart, Ainsley, and the family celebrates. Hugh has difficulty stepping into Lance's shoes and running Lance's businesses after Lance goes to prison. These more intimate looks at family life outside the courtroom reiterate that, ultimately, this book is about two families: the Malcos and the Rudys.

The book's discussion of family focuses primarily on the father-son relationships between Jesse and Keith and between Lance and Hugh. In both cases, the father-son relationship is strong and characterized by intense loyalty. Hugh is so loyal to Lance that when Jesse puts Lance in prison, Hugh orchestrates the attack on Jesse. Even after Jesse is dead, Hugh's "victory" of killing the man is marred by his father's being in prison: "For Hugh, the occasion was bittersweet. He was delighted Jesse Rudy was gone, but so was his father. Lance should be dining with them and savoring the moment" (316). Meanwhile, Keith is so loyal to Jesse that when Jesse is killed, he makes it his top priority to seek vengeance—and not only have Hugh convicted but also make sure that he gets the death penalty.

In addition, these chapters reiterate the significance of the media relative to law, order, and public opinion. As soon as Lance pleads guilty, it's reported in the *Gulf Coast Register*: "MALCO PLEADS GUILTY—ORDERED TO PRISON" (287). Jesse is undoubtedly happy to have his "win" widely reported for all to hear about. After Jesse's death, another media frenzy ensues, with sensational headlines like: "JESSE RUDY KILLED IN COURTHOUSE EXPLOSION," "MOB STRIKES BACK—PROSECUTOR DEAD," and "CRUSADING DA KILLED IN BILOXI" (320). The media seemingly embraces the hero/villain, good-guy/bad-guy, DA/mob dichotomy. However, the narrative reveals more about the characters—in particular, some of Jesse's less morally upstanding moments—and that the reality isn't "black-and-white," highlighting the theme of **Morality Versus Legality**.

These chapters lay the groundwork for the book's climax: Hugh's conviction for Jesse's murder and his subsequent execution. The FBI, led by Agent Lewis, investigates Henry Taylor ("Lyle") and sets a trap for him that ultimately results in his arrest—as well as Nevin's and Hugh's. It's an intricate operation that plays out over multiple chapters and months of time within the narrative. This helps show how difficult it can be to actually catch and convict criminals. Knowing that someone did something illegal is one thing; proving it is another.

These chapters attest to the power of an omniscient, third-person narrator. Keith is unaware of the complex investigation that the FBI is conducting. After talking to Judge Oliphant about his suspicions that the Malcos were behind the murder, he doesn't have much hope of ever catching them. The Judge tells him, "Contract killings are virtually impossible because the guilty party touches nothing" (332). However, the third-person narration reveals otherwise. If the book were narrated in the first person (for example, by Keith or Hugh), these details wouldn't be available.

Part 3, Chapters 43-50

Part 3: "The Prisoners"

Part 3, Chapter 43 Summary

Keith is appointed the new DA, stepping into Jesse's shoes. Meanwhile, Hugh visits Lance in prison: "They talked about everything but the obvious. Jesse Rudy's death was never mentioned. Lance had not been involved in it, and he was worried that his unpredictable son had done something stupid" (339). The FBI continues to trail Henry Taylor and has placed wiretaps on his phones. They learn that he's in financial trouble.

Part 3, Chapter 44 Summary

Keith starts his job as DA. The holiday season arrives, and the Rudy family gets together to celebrate—the first time without Jesse. During Christmas, Keith and Ainsley (his wife) announce that she's pregnant. Agnes is ecstatic: "When she heard the wonderful news that she'd be a grandmother, she finally broke down. The emotion was contagious, and in an instant the entire family was having a good cry. Tears of joy" (346).

Part 3, Chapter 45 Summary

Henry Taylor is approached by a private investigator, J. W. Gross, who wants him to carry out a hit on behalf of one of his clients. Henry is unaware that J. W. Gross is working for the FBI. This is all part of the FBI's plan to capture Henry Taylor and then coerce him to testify against Hugh and Nevin. The scheme goes as planned. By the end of the chapter, both Henry Taylor and Nevin have been arrested.

Part 3, Chapter 46 Summary

FBI Agent Lewis gives Keith the good news: "We have in custody the man who killed your father" (361). With Henry Taylor and Nevin in custody, the FBI gets the additional information they need to arrest Hugh Malco.

Part 3, Chapter 47 Summary

Keith, now 28, announces the indictments of Henry Taylor and Nevin to the media: "The indictment charges that on August 20 of last year, 1976, Nevin, and Henry Taylor did conspire to commit and died indeed commit the murder of Jesse Rudy. Nevin paid a large sum of money to Henry Taylor to carry out the contract killing" (364). Shortly thereafter, Hugh is indicted for capital murder. On February 18, all three men appear before a judge, and all three plead "not guilty." The narrator describes Keith and Hugh, standing in the same courtroom on opposite sides: "The two had once been the same size. In their glory days as twelve-year-old stars they were roughly the same height and weight, though no one bothered to measure back then. As they grew, their genes took charge" (369).

Part 3, Chapter 48 Summary

Bail hearings are set for the prisoners. None of them are given the option of bail. Keith approaches Henry's lawyer and cuts a deal: If Henry agrees to cooperate with the State (to testify against Nevin and Hugh) and pleads guilty, he'll serve only 10 years. Before the trial for Nevin and Hugh can commence, Keith's colleagues convince him to step back from the case as prosecuting DA because of his personal connection to the case. Keith agrees. Another lawyer, Chuck McClure, takes on the case: "He had sent more men to death row than any other prosecutor in the state's history" (377).

Part 3, Chapter 49 Summary

Nevin is offered a plea deal: Testify against Hugh, and he'll get a lighter sentence. His lawyer advises him to take it. Otherwise, Nevin will likely get the maximum penalty and die in prison. Nevin is the only person who can concretely link Hugh to the murder. Nevin's lawyer tells Keith, "You desperately need Noll because no one else can pin all the blame on Malco. [...] Assuming Malco ordered the hit, no one else can prove it" (382).

Part 3, Chapter 50 Summary

Hugh's trial begins. It's a media circus: "The murder of Jesse Rudy was the most sensational in the history of the Gulf Coast" (388). Henry and Nevin both testify. The jury deliberates for only 47 minutes before finding Hugh guilty of capital murder. The next day, sentencing begins. Keith's mother, Agnes, testifies, talking about how much she misses her husband. Hugh's mother, Carmen, also testifies: "Joshua Burch [Hugh's lawyer] had convinced [Carmen] that she was the only person who might be able to save her son's life" (398). The plan doesn't work. Hugh is given the death sentence.

Part 3, Chapters 43-50 Analysis

The chapters after Jesse's death further elucidate the theme of **Familial Identity and Legacy**, especially in the context of father-son relationships. First, Keith takes over the role of DA, literally following in his father's footsteps. Keith fixates on the idea of avenging his father's death, fulfilling a common trope in literature, television, and film: "You killed my father/mother and must pay." Examples range from *Harry Potter* to *The Lion King*. Ironically, Jesse's death occurred for similar reasons—as Hugh ordered the hit on Jesse in revenge for his locking Lance away. Jesse didn't kill Lance, but in Hugh's eyes he may as well have; Lance essentially ceases to exist in the "real world" while he's behind bars.

Keith's loyalty to Jesse, and Hugh's loyalty to Lance, are unquestionable. However, the narrative casts doubt on the logic of this loyalty, hinting at the question of whether it's right to blindly follow and support another person, perhaps even breaking laws or doing immoral things, even if that person is a father. Lance himself doesn't seem impressed by Hugh's vengeful acts. In fact, he sees them in a different light altogether: "Jesse's death was never mentioned. Lance had not been involved in it, and he was worried that his unpredictable son had done something stupid" (339).

These chapters further the narrative's criticism of corruption—and its argument that corruption and greed often go hand in hand. Fats exemplified this, ignoring crime in Biloxi in exchange for payments and perks. Now, the connection between corruption, criminal activity, and greed is exemplified by the FBI's pursuit of Henry Taylor. When the FBI learns that he's in a financial crisis, they leverage the situation, setting up a sting operation and luring him in with a fake hit job—one that pays a lot of money. Henry's primary motivation for killing people is clearly money, a testimony to the lengths to which people will go when fulfilling their greed.

The pinnacle of action in these chapters is Hugh's guilty verdict, the final plot point in Part 3. Hugh is not only declared guilty but also sentenced to death. Part 4, "The Row" (referring to death row) takes place as Hugh awaits his demise. His receiving the death penalty introduces the potential for discussions about its morality—which Part 4 explores further. The story hints at the complex moral dispute surrounding the death penalty when Keith agrees to allow another lawyer, Chuck McClure, to prosecute Hugh's case; the narrative notes, "[Chuck] had sent more men to death row than any other prosecutor in the state's history" (377). The implicit question is whether this is a good thing. In Keith's eyes, it apparently is.

Although much of the content in these chapters focuses on the legal details of Hugh's trial, the author is careful to reiterate repeatedly that at its heart this legal thriller is a story about two families. The Rudy family recovers from Jesse's loss, and Keith and Ainsley announce her pregnancy. Agnes's emotional reaction to the pregnancy is a reminder that Jesse's death isn't just about a DA being killed by the mob and all the sensational headlines that brings; it's about sons and daughters losing a father and a wife losing her husband. The narrative reiterates this reality when Agnes testifies at Hugh's sentencing, talking about her loss. Carmen offers the counterpoint in her testimony as a mother who experiences the shock of her son's being sentenced to death.

These chapters reiterate the significance of friendships, not just familial relationships, as well. When Keith and Hugh appear in the same courtroom, the book reflects on their shared path—and their splintered future: "The two had once been the same size. In their glory days as twelve-year-old stars they were roughly the same height and weight, though no one bothered to measure back then. As they grew, their genes took charge" (369). The narrative then describes how the two boys have grown up to be *physically* different, but the mention of "genes" points to the families: Each boy followed his respective path, essentially predetermined for him by his family. This familial loyalty put them on opposite sides of good and evil, and pitted them against one another.

Part 4, Chapters 51-59

Part 4: "The Row"

Part 4, Chapter 51 Summary

The Rudy family celebrates the birth of Ainsley's second child in January 1979. Meanwhile, the Malco family is immersed in Hugh's appeals process. Lance visits Hugh on death row, known simply as "The Row" to inmates. Hugh tells Lance about the man in the cell next to his, Jimmy Lee Gray, who raped and killed a three-year-old girl. Hugh also tells Lance, "Death row is the safest place in prison. There's no contact with other inmates" (405).

Part 4, Chapter 52 Summary

Hugh's appeal is denied when the Mississippi Supreme Court upholds his conviction in 1980. Meanwhile, Keith gets a letter from Haley, who's still in prison: Haley tells Keith that he has information about a drug trafficking operation that implicates Fats. Keith turns the information over to the FBI and the Drug Enforcement Agency, and Fats is arrested and sentenced to 20 years in prison. Before he's sent away, however, he dies by suicide.

Part 4, Chapter 53 Summary

Keith, having effectively completed Jesse's mission to "clean up the Coast," becomes bored with the DA job. Hugh, Lance, and Fats are all out of the picture. Keith announces that he's running for the state's Attorney General office. The *Gulf Coast Register* endorses his campaign, as do other southern newspapers. Keith wins the election and, at just 35, becomes "the youngest AG in the state's history, and the youngest in the country" (418).

Part 4, Chapter 54 Summary

Following a 1976 capital punishment appeals case, the US Court "gave the green light for the death states to resume killing. Most did so with great enthusiasm" (419). The first person Mississippi brings to the gas chamber is Jimmy Lee Gray, the man in the cell next to Hugh's: "Far from a swift and painless death, the execution was botched and it was clear that Gray suffered greatly" (420). On "The Row," the prisoners' mood shifts: The men become more apprehensive, realizing that they may actually face execution and that it may be painful. Meanwhile, Nevin, under the alias "Lou Palmer" (to protect him, since he cooperated in Hugh's case) is still in prison and is making plans to escape with the help of another inmate, Sammy Shaw.

Part 4, Chapter 55 Summary

In 1984, Keith is sworn in as Mississippi's Attorney General. As AG, he's eager to fast-track Hugh's execution. At the same time, Henry Taylor— the man who actually planted the bomb that killed Jesse—is doing his time, protected with false alibis and frequent relocations to different prisons (part of the deal he got with law enforcement in exchange for cooperating in the case against Hugh). However, Lance figures out Henry's real identity and where to find him and orders a hit on him. The men who do the job then dispose of Henry's body in the ocean, for the sharks to eat—however, they first take a photo of Henry's dead body, hanging over the ocean water. Lance has a copy of the photo sent to "Lou Palmer" (aka Nevin) as a threat, which underscores the theme of **The Dangers of Loyalty**.

Part 4, Chapter 56 Summary

Keith attends another of Hugh's appeals hearings. His hope is that "Hugh Malco would be strapped down while Keith was still attorney general" (435). Meanwhile, Lance is out of prison and struggling to adapt to civilian life: "He was sixty-two years old. [...] His favorite son was on death row. His marriage was long gone. Though he still had plenty of assets, his empire was in serious decline. His friends had deserted him. [...] The Malco name, once feared and respected by man, was mud" (435-36).

Part 4, Chapter 57 Summary

Nevin and Sammy escape prison. Sammy is captured quickly. Nevin manages to escape completely. Keith isn't worried, knowing that Nevin will flee far to get away from Lance, now free: "The last place Noll would surface was the Coast. Lance had put a $50,000 contract on his head and he'd made sure Noll knew it. If he had good sense, which he did, he would find his way to Brazil" (442).

Part 4, Chapter 58 Summary

Hugh's series of appeals continue. Finally, the last appeal is finished, without success, and the execution date is set: March 28, midnight, 1985. A media frenzy ensues after the announcement:

> The *Gulf Coast Register* re-ran the old team photo of Keith and Hugh as Little League all-stars, and the background proved irresistible. Stories flourished about their childhood on the Point. Former coaches, teachers, friends, and teammates were tracked down and interviewed (443).

Hugh's last chance is an appeal to the governor of Mississippi, who could issue clemency. However, the governor approaches Keith first to discuss the topic, asking Keith how he feels about it. Keith tells him, "I want him [Hugh] executed" (445).

Part 4, Chapter 59 Summary

On the evening of Hugh's execution, Keith goes to visit Hugh on The Row. The governor lets Keith borrow his Lear jet for the trip. On the way to the meeting, Keith flashes back to his and Hugh's shared childhood. During Keith and Hugh's conversation on The Row, Hugh tells Keith that he didn't mean to kill Jesse—the bomb was only meant to scare him. Hugh even cries. Keith believes him. Hugh reveals that he doesn't want Lance or his mother there for his execution: "I can't stand the thought of either of my parents watching me die like this" (453). Keith won't stay to watch either, telling Hugh: "For a long time, I've dreamed of watching your execution, but I can't do it. I'm flying to Biloxi to sit with my mother" (454). Hugh replies, "So long, pal. I'll see you on the other side" (454).

Part 4, Chapters 51-59 Analysis

The book's final part focuses on the runup to Hugh's execution and is entitled "The Row," after his time on Death Row. The narrative includes details regarding Hugh's multiple appeals and his request for clemency from the governor of Mississippi. In addition, the narrative discusses the US Supreme Court Case that allowed Mississippi and other "death states" to proceed with executions after they were paused nationwide for a period. The author's decision to include these details opens up the debate regarding the morality of capital punishment—which morality is thrown into doubt simply by the fact that it's often disputed in the US Court system.

The author includes the case of Jimmy Lee Gray to further tease out this moral conundrum. This tiny subplot serves no other purpose; it doesn't drive the narrative further significantly. However, it exemplifies the difficulty of this moral conundrum: Jimmy Lee has committed an atrocious crime, raping and killing a three-year-old child. The question is whether another human has the right to kill him as a result. By showing that the execution is botched and Jimmy's death is thus excruciatingly painful, the author makes the question even tougher. The narrative doesn't spare any details regarding either Jimmy's crime or his death. These extremes complicate the morality question surrounding the death penalty even further. However, the narrative never offers a clear opinion regarding whether the death penalty is moral.

However, one character has a very clear opinion on the topic: Keith. Part of what drives Keith's ambition to become AG is fast-tracking Hugh's execution. When the Governor considers Hugh's plea for clemency and discusses it with Keith, Keith simply replies, "I want him executed" (445). This conversation speaks to the book's argument regarding corruption. Keith's personal influence with the governor arguably helps speed Hugh's execution. Ideally, a fair justice system wouldn't allow this kind of personal influence, especially in such serious life-or-death questions.

In addition to examining the morality of capital punishment, which foregrounds the theme of **Morality Versus Legality**, the book's final part looks at some of the other complexities and challenges of the US legal system. Lance is one example. Like many inmates, he finds rehabilitation difficult after he's released from prison. While he was away, his life fell into shambles:

He was sixty-two years old. [...] His favorite son was on death row. His marriage was long gone. Though he still had plenty of assets, his empire was in serious decline. His friends had deserted him. [...] The Malco name, once feared and respected by man, was mud (435-36).

The book concludes by bringing the focus back to the novel's namesakes: the boys from Biloxi. Hugh and Keith are thrust into the spotlight, as a media storm surrounds their childhood friendship: "The *Gulf Coast Register* re-ran the old team photo of Keith and Hugh as Little League all-stars, and the background proved irresistible. Stories flourished about their childhood on the Point. Former coaches, teachers, friends, and teammates were tracked down and interviewed" (443). The book ends with the last conversation between Hugh and Keith. Even at the end, they have no animosity toward one another. Keith almost feels sympathy for Hugh, while Hugh's final words to Keith (and the last in the book) are, "So long, pal. I'll see you on the other side" (454).

Character Analysis

Keith Rudy

The closest character the narrative has to a "protagonist"—though a morally questionable one at times—is Keith, one of the Biloxi "boys." The narrative starts by aligning him with his childhood friend Hugh, emphasizing their similarities:

Their families lived two streets apart. Their parents and grandparents knew each other well. They went to the same Catholic church, the same schools, played in the same streets, sandlots, and beaches, and fished with their fathers in the Gulf on lazy weekends (8).

However, the boys' paths eventually diverge. Keith follows the path of his father, Jesse, becoming a lawyer and, later, assuming Jesse's DA position after his death. It's when Keith starts to come into this position of power that he starts to show morally dubious traits—a hint that power can corrupt. Keith's mission to avenge his father's death drives the remainder of the narrative. It also drives his own rise to power; for example, he's determined to become AG so that he can speed Hugh's execution. The idea of pursuing political office in the interest of killing another man is uncomfortable, if not downright abhorrent. Keith's bloodlust becomes even more questionable when Hugh petitions the governor for clemency. When the governor consults Keith on the topic, Keith says: "I want him executed" (445). All this becomes even more troubling after his final conversation with Hugh, when Hugh reveals that he never intended to kill Jesse.

Keith's character thus speaks to the theme of **The Dangers of Loyalty** . He's so loyal to his father, even in death, and so intent on following in his father's footsteps, that he doesn't leave any space or opportunity for a different path. Keith's world boils down to a focused desire for revenge—which may not be the best answer, as he realizes after his final conversation with Hugh. He can't even watch the execution: "For a long time, I've dreamed of watching your execution, but I can't do it. I'm flying to Biloxi to sit with my mother" (454). By the book's end, he seems poised to rise to the top—having gone from being the DA to being the country's youngest AG. Governor may be next. The problem is, Keith won't in any way break the cycle of corruption in power. Already, he has used a personal connection (to the governor) to influence whether a man on death row should get clemency, in effect singlehandedly putting Hugh to death. His inability to remove his personal point of view from his actions when given a position of power suggests that he'll be just as corruptible as others who came before him.

Jesse Rudy

Keith's father, Jesse, is the other "good guy" in the book, setting the path that Keith follows. However, Jesse is likewise not 100% pure; in fact, his character seems to embody the phrase, "Die a hero or live long enough to see yourself become the villain." The narrative clearly paints Jesse's trajectory from purely a "good guy" to a morally questionable character. As a young lawyer, he has such a polished reputation that others approach him to run for DA to "clean up the Coast" (61). At this point, Jesse's family's safety is his priority, and he declines. Later, however, he changes his mind. In his first DA race, Jesse still plays by the rules: When Jesse informs the current DA, Rex Dubisson, of his plans to challenge him by running for DA. Rex warns him, "There's nothing clean about politics around here, Jesse. You're being naive. It's a dirty game," to which Jesse replies, "It doesn't have to be" (114). However, later Jesse is no longer so adamant, resorting to plenty of dirty tactics himself.

The most poignant example of Jesse's fall from grace as "the good guy" comes when he extorts Lance to force him into a plea deal involving prison time. Joshua, Lance's lawyer, tells Jesse, "This is ruthless" (284) and calls his tactic "blackmail," implying that it isn't just morally questionable—it's also illegal. Jesse has essentially become a criminal in his attempts to put another criminal behind bars. However, this all remains secret, and Jesse is lauded as the DA who helped "clean up the Coast" (61) in the book. In death, he becomes a martyr of sorts; even though he wasn't the perfect good guy, the general public isn't aware of it. This highlights the book's argument that the good/evil dichotomy is generally overly simplistic. In reality, most people operate in moral gray areas, as Jesse exemplifies.

Hugh Malco

Keith's counterpoint in the narrative, Hugh, is the other Biloxi "boy." While Keith goes the path of the "good guy" (though no white knight himself), Hugh goes that of the "bad guy," falling into the criminal underworld like his father, Lance. He gives up baseball in favor of boxing, starts hanging around his dad's clubs, and accompanies Nevin on missions to beat people up—all while still a teenager. Hugh's zealous desire to follow in Lance's footsteps leads to his death; he's executed for arranging Jesse's hit. The book foreshadows Hugh's demise early on: "Career gangsters like Lance Malco went to prison, or took a bullet, or they died in prison. That was Hugh's future too" (170).

Hugh's story serves as a cautionary tale about the dangers of unquestioning loyalty and insistent adherence to familial legacy. Lance had the money and means to arrange any number of other paths for Hugh—he could have gone to college and become a lawyer like Keith, theoretically. However, the father needed someone to whom he could pass his empire to, and the son was the logical choice. The narrative paints Hugh as a bit of a fool; his own father doesn't even have confidence in his abilities. With Lance facing prison time, he knows he needs to make plans for his businesses: "Hugh was confident he could run the businesses in his father's absence. His father wasn't so sure" (269). It's troubling that the devoted son, eager to earn his father's approval, doesn't seem to have his father's confidence.

Lance Malco

The book's antagonist, the main "bad guy" in the narrative, is Lance. From the start, he clearly has no issue with violence, including murder, to protect his businesses and his reputation. For example, in Chapter 10, Lance arranges for the intimidation of Marcus Dean Poppy and the murder of Earl Fortier, after the two cheat him out of a club deal. This is just one of many instances in which Lance participates in what is essentially gang warfare. However, Lance never gets his hands dirty, always relying on Nevin to do the grunt work, like contracting hitmen. This exemplifies the book's point about how hard it is to shake corruption; the people at the top always have underlings to protect them.

Lance seems eager for Hugh to follow in his footsteps early on: "Hugh was only sixteen but was mature for his age and could certainly take care of himself. He was showing no interest in college and that was fine with Lance as well. The boy was needed in the family business" (102). Just like Jesse and Keith's dynamic, the father essentially charts out the son's path. Hugh is just as loyal to Lance as Keith is to Jesse. The book again calls this level of loyalty into question when Hugh has Jesse killed in revenge for Lance's imprisonment. Even Lance seems to question Hugh's extreme loyalty: "They [Lance and Hugh] talked about everything but the obvious. Jesse Rudy's death was never mentioned. Lance had not been involved in it, and he was worried that his unpredictable son had done something stupid" (339).

Nevin Noll

Nevin is Lance's main henchman—the guy who does his dirty work. After Lance goes to jail, Nevin supports Hugh as his second-in-command. Nevin's character demonstrates how crime and corruption tend to continue unchecked because the people in charge of criminal operations always have "middlemen" to take care of criminal acts. For example, it's Nevin who deals directly with the hitmen that Lance (and later Hugh) engage. Judge Oliphant confirms how this approach—never allowing "the boss," the man in charge, to have any direct contact in such deals— protects them: "Contract killings are virtually impossible because the guilty party touches nothing" (332).

However, having henchmen do one's dirty work only works if they remain loyal. Nevin is initially loyal to the Malcos but ultimately turns against them, betraying Hugh by testifying in his trial and confirming that Hugh was the one who had the idea to take out a hit on Jesse. Nevin's character thus speaks to the book's theme of **The Dangers of Loyalty.**

Ginger Redfield

Ginger's character primarily serves as a plot device, in varying ways. First, she's one of Lance's competitors, helping demonstrate how cutthroat the world of crime can get. This is also evident in more minor characters, like Dusty Cromwell (Lance pays someone to burn down Dusty's bar; Dusty has the arsonist killed and sends his ear to Lance in the mail). More significantly, Ginger is one of Jesse's first points of attack in his crusade to "clean up the Coast" (61). She serves as an example to Lance of what he may face if Jesse is successful in his crusade.

Additionally, Ginger's case serves another purpose: to help explicate the legal details of the "nuisance law" that Jesse uses successfully to go after Lance. The trial affords in-depth insights into proceedings like jury selection; in Ginger's case, jury tampering results in a mistrial and Ginger walking free. This highlights why jury selection is so significant to a case's outcome. Finally, Ginger's case helps demonstrate the tediousness of the appeals process. It takes almost two years from the time that the appeal is initiated for the courts to rule on it—and only then does the Carousel close, for good. By using Ginger's case to illustrate these details, the author provides some rudimentary legal knowledge that enables a clearer focus on the dramatics of Lance's subsequent trial.

Sheriff Albert "Fats" Bowman

One of the book's major focuses is the inherent and deep nature of corruption in society—especially in areas where corruption really shouldn't occur, including law enforcement, the criminal justice system, and politics. Ironically, the societal systems created to fight corruption often create it. "Fats" epitomizes the rampant nature of corruption in the world. He not only takes money from known criminals but is even actively involved in drug running. In this way, Fats further demonstrates how corruption is often motivated by greed, money, and selfishness.

More shocking still is that everybody seems well aware of his corruption. Even the governor of Mississippi knows; he tells Keith and Jesse, "Fats Bowman belongs in prison" (244). That said, Fats is only one of many corrupt characters in the novel (besides those actively engaged in criminal activities, like Lance, Hugh, Nevin, and the various hitmen they work with). Jesse and Keith are "good guys" but exhibit some questionable behavior. Even lawyers, like Joshua Burch—who works for Lance—are corrupt. For example, Joshua urges Lance, "Go see Cyrus Knapp, the heart doctor. He's a quack but he'll do what I say. Tell him since you got arrested you've been having chest pains, dizziness, fatigue" (268). The lawyer has no qualms essentially falsifying medical records.

Themes

Familial Identity and Legacy

The Boys from Biloxi is a legal thriller. However, it's ultimately a story about two families, the Malco and Rudy clans. Themes of familial identity and legacy are prevalent in the story, starting with the depiction of the families' histories. Both families are of Croatian descent and have immigrant backgrounds. Both are, in their own ways, immigrant "success stories" (a problematic and outdated label because classifying immigrants into "successful" versus "unsuccessful" can lead to anti-immigrant sentiment). Lance becomes the biggest crime boss on The Strip, while Jesse becomes a successful lawyer, the first local lawyer of Croatian descent—and a legend of sorts: "Jesse Rudy's success became the source of many proud stories on the Point" (28).

In this story, familial identity is intrinsically tied to the family business. Professionally, both Hugh and Keith follow in their father's footsteps. Lance explicates this specifically when he sees Hugh getting involved in his clubs as a teenager: "[Hugh] was showing no interest in college and that was fine with Lance as well. The boy was needed in the family business" (102). Meanwhile, Keith picks up Jesse's "crusade" to "clean up the Coast" (61). For both the Malco and Rudy families, the family business is male-dominated; this helps emphasize the strong bond between father and son in each case. Both Lance and Jesse look to their sons to carry on the family legacy, from the business standpoint. Meanwhile, the narrative suggests, it's up to the women in the family to carry on the legacy biologically by having babies. The story hints at this other form of familial legacy when Ainsley (Keith's wife) announces her pregnancy: "When [Agnes; Jesse's wife and Keith's mother] heard the wonderful news that she would be a grandmother, she finally broke down. The emotion was contagious, and in an instant the entire family was having a good cry. Tears of joy" (346).

Although the bulk of the book's plot centers on the "legal thriller" aspects of chasing and prosecuting criminals (and the criminals dodging these efforts), the author provides constant reminders that the narrative is ultimately about family. Throughout the novel, he mentions major milestones, such as Keith's graduation from college and his marriage to Ainsley. The announcement of Ainsley's pregnancy is another example. The author also includes less happy personal anecdotes, such as

Carmen's and Lance's divorce. By providing these personal insights into the Rudy and Malco families' lives, the narrative emphasizes that it's about personal relationships—families and friendships—not just crime.

The Dangers of Loyalty

Lance and Jesse each carve out their own path to success. Their sons then follow those paths, which their fathers have set out for them, attesting to the importance of familial identity, legacy, and heritage. This pursuit of family legacy and devotion to heritage requires great loyalty. Both Hugh and Keith are painstakingly loyal to their families—more specifically, to their fathers. As a result, their friendship suffers. It's after Keith learns of Jesse's plan to run for DA (which Keith supports) that Keith and Hugh have their last beer together: "[Keith] acted as though all was well, but he knew that these moments were fleeting. The friendships were about to change, or vanish altogether. [...] For him and Hugh, it was probably their last beer together" (108). Familial loyalty, in this case, trumps the loyalty of friendship.

The narrative doesn't necessarily paint this extreme level of familial loyalty as a good thing, however. Hugh's story in particular demonstrates the dangers of taking loyalty too far. To avenge Lance's being sent to prison, he takes out a hit on Jesse, gets caught, and ends up on death row. Hugh may think he's being loyal, but Lance thinks he's being stupid: "They talked about everything but the obvious. Jesse Rudy's death was never mentioned. Lance had not been involved in it, and he was worried that his unpredictable son had done something stupid" (339). The narrative shows that unquestioningly following another person, for any reason—even if they're family—isn't wise and can result in poor decision making.

Nonetheless, familial loyalty seems to be the only kind of loyalty that holds steady in the narrative. Other types of loyalty, such as the loyalty of a friend or an employee, are less reliable. Lance experiences this when Nevin, his managers, and the waitresses who worked in his bars all turn on him. Once he's no longer providing them with cash and protection, their loyalty wanes. In particular, Nevin, Lance's main henchman, presents a different angle on the dangers of loyalty—the fact that you can't always rely on someone's staying true to you. Even a seemingly loyal person can be a betrayer. In the case of men like Nevin, loyalty is bought. Nevin—and others, like Henry Taylor ("Lyle") and even the sex workers in Lance's bars—take money in exchange for their loyalty. These people all end up turning. Only loyalty informed by blood ties, like the loyalty Keith and Hugh show their fathers, seems untouchable (at least in the narrative—in reality, this isn't always true, given that families turn on one another as well).

Morality Versus Legality

As a legal thriller that deals with crime, *The Boys from Biloxi* inherently deals with questions of legality. Discussions of legality often intertwine with questions of morality. In simplistic terms, people want to believe in the dichotomy of moral/immoral; ideally, a criminal justice system reflects that dichotomy through rules on what's legal/illegal. However, in reality, things aren't so "black and white." Many of the actions the book's characters take attest to this fact. Jesse is the prime example. He's painted as the book's white knight, the good-guy DA who's committed to "cleaning up" the area and eliminating dangerous crime. However, Jesse takes immoral and illegal actions to meet his goals—for instance, when he traps Lance into a plea bargain. As Joshua tells Jesse at the time, his actions are "ruthless" and amount to "blackmail" (285). The question is whether can Jesse's immoral/illegal actions are forgivable because they're (presumably) in the interest of the greater good—locking away a dangerous crime boss like Lance, who's responsible for killings as well as illegal drug trades and sex work (including of minors—Cindy, the girl who Hugh falls for, is only 15). This conundrum exemplifies how judging people based on "black-and-white," "good-versus-bad" categorizations of their actions is often too simplistic.

The book also raises the morality versus legality question in its discussion of capital punishment. The author is a vocal critic of the death penalty; however, the novel merely presents the question of whether the death penalty is right or wrong, leaving it open for consideration. The case of Jimmy Lee Gray brings the issue to a head, and the narrative presents two extremes to pose a complex and troubling question. First, the reader learns about Gray's crime: He raped and murdered his girlfriend's three-year-old daughter—and admits to other rapes—so, presumably, there's no question of his guilt. This is an immoral man who has committed a terrible crime against another human being. The question, however, is whether another human then has the right to kill him as punishment. The author complicates this question by portraying a botched execution. Gray unquestionably endures considerable pain when the execution goes awry. Thus, observers who support the death penalty might second-guess their choice. The capital punishment question epitomizes how morality/legality are intertwined because numerous court cases—

including a Supreme Court case mentioned in the book—have debated whether the death penalty should be allowed; thus, legal cases are made on the basis of moral judgments.

Symbols & Motifs

Baseball

A recurring motif, symbolizing purity and an "All American" type of simplicity, is baseball. At the beginning of the book, when "the boys" are young, it's one of the things that binds Keith and Hugh together. The boys play in the same league and are both above-average players, making their parents proud. Baseball has been called "America's National Pastime" and has generally been associated, especially in the past, with American ideals of wholesomeness and purity. The fact that two sons from immigrant families embrace the sport speaks to their efforts to integrate into their new homeland (something that's evident even in the way their family names are adapted, from "Malokovic" to "Malco" and "Rudic" to "Rudy").

Later, as the boys grow up, they leave their love of baseball behind. Keith seems to drop the sport as he focuses on his academic endeavors. Hugh gives up baseball and picks up boxing, which is far more violent, reflecting his increasing participation in the violence of the criminal underworld. The boys' dropping baseball parallels their transition to adulthood: Their lives become less wholesome and more complex, and they deal with issues like family identity, paternal loyalty, and murder and vengeance. The book's last passages recall the boys' wholesome beginnings: In the media hubbub leading up to Hugh's execution, "The *Gulf Coast Register* re-ran the old team photo of Keith and Hugh as Little League all-stars, and the background proved irresistible. Stories flourished about their childhood on the Point. Former coaches, teachers, friends, and teammates were tracked down and interviewed" (443). It's a sad reminder of the boys' simple lives as kids as well as the fact that they used to play, literally, on the same team.

The Insurance Companies

One major subplot in the second part of the book, "The Crusader," is Jesse's battle against the insurance companies following Hurricane Camille. The insurers are the ultimate symbol of corrupt capitalist greed, using a technicality to avoid paying everyday people the money they're owed to rebuild their businesses and their homes. By taking on the insurance companies, Jesse casts himself as David in a David-versus-Goliath type of battle: the smaller good guy against the behemoth of evil. However, Jesse's actions aren't totally selfless. He knows that this will help him win favor with the locals, improving his odds of a future DA race win.

Still, the corruption of the insurance companies is paramount. While they don't help regular people, they do help Lance and the other crime bosses get back on their feet—thanks to Lance's clout, connections, and cash. After a disaster like Camille, the age-old adage "the rich get richer and the poor get poorer" seems to hold true. Although Jesse ultimately helps people get their payouts, it's a momentous effort, requiring multiple trials and appeals before people see their money. The insurers are yet another example of the deep corruption at every level of society.

The Media

Furthering the exploration of corruption, the book depicts the use of media to distort public opinion. The most obvious example of media use for personal gain is the smear campaign Jesse engages in when running for DA. He uses mailings to attack the club owners, while his opponents use mailings to portray Jesse as being "soft on crime"—not a desirable trait in a DA. The direct mailings become such a mud-slinging mess that a judge rules against them to stop them. In addition to the direct mailings, which are privately created media, the public media even supports a sort of corruption. For example, when Lance is indicted, Keith personally contacts the *Gulf Coast Register* to inform them. It's important to Keith and Jesse that the public recognizes their "win." Later, when Lance takes the plea, the *Gulf Coast Register* reports: "MALCO PLEADS GUILTY—ORDERED TO PRISON" (287). Jesse is undoubtedly happy to have his "win" widely reported for all to hear about.

These instances highlight the undeniable role of media in the interplay of politics, crime, the legal system, and public opinion. Ideally, newspapers report facts honestly and accurately, without bias. However, this isn't the reality portrayed in the book. Jesse and Keith in particular are adept at using the media to their advantage. Even Jesse's death is portrayed in sensationalist terms, with headlines like "JESSE RUDY KILLED IN COURTHOUSE EXPLOSION," "MOB STRIKES BACK—PROSECUTOR DEAD," and "CRUSADING DA KILLED IN BILOXI" (320). Keith uses the media to his advantage when the men behind Jesse's murder are captured, holding a press conference to announce it: "The indictment charges that on August

20 of last year, 1976, Nevin, and Henry Taylor did conspire to commit and did indeed commit the murder of Jesse Rudy. Nevin paid a large sum of money to Henry Taylor to carry out the contract killing" (364).

The media further distorts reality by embracing the hero/villain, good-guy/bad-guy, DA/mob dichotomy. The narrative reveals more about the characters—in particular, some of Jesse's less morally upstanding moments—so this dichotomy isn't as "black-and-white." Still, as the portrayal of Jesse as a hero in death illustrates, the media insists on sensational headlines and stories—even until the bitter end, when it picks up on the old friendship between Keith and Hugh:

The *Gulf Coast Register* re-ran the old team photo of Keith and Hugh as Little League all-stars, and the background proved irresistible. Stories flourished about their childhood on the Point. Former coaches, teachers, friends, and teammates were tracked down and interviewed (443).

Important Quotes

1. "The biggest obstacle facing any attempts at reform was the longtime corruption of the police and elected officials."
(Part 1, Chapter 1, Page 5)

These words lay the groundwork for the battle of "good" versus "evil" in the book. Jesse's crusade against crime along the coast could be straightforward if not for the deeply ingrained corruption summarized in this quote.

2. "Their families lived two streets apart. Their parents and grandparents knew each other well. They went to the same Catholic church, the same schools, played in the same streets, sandlots, and beaches, and fished with their fathers in the Gulf on lazy weekends."
(Part 1, Chapter 2, Page 8)

Hugh and Keith, "The Boys from Biloxi," are ultimately on different sides of the fight against crime. However, they start out in the same place. This quote emphasizes the similarities of the boys' early lives, when they are friends, before their paths diverge.

3. "Jesse had no interest in jeopardizing the safety of his family [...] But once planted, the idea would not go away."
(Part 1, Chapter 8, Page 62)

These words depict Jesse's thoughts when others first suggest that he run for DA. His fears regarding safety are ultimately justified when he's killed because of his work as DA.

4. "Poor young Pat Graebel stood at the podium, the butt of the joke, the fool of the hour, the hotshot prosecutor whose case had vanished into thin air."
(Part 1, Chapter 11, Pages 92 - 93)

The depiction of this criminal case, shown early in the narrative, before Jesse is DA, reiterates how difficult it will be for Jesse to "clean up the Coast" (61). Pat Graebel seems to have an easy case to win—but then witnesses start disappearing or not cooperating. This exemplifies the deep criminal corruption that Jesse will take on.

5. "Hugh was only sixteen but was mature for his age and could certainly take care of himself. He was showing no interest in college and that was fine with Lance as well. The boy was needed in the family business."
(Part 1, Chapter 12, Page 102)

*These words depict Lance's views on his son, Hugh. They speak to loyalty and the book's theme of **Familial Identity and Legacy**. Some fathers might not want their son pursuing a life of crime; for Lance, however, it's just a matter of taking over the family business.*

6. "[Keith] acted as though all was well, but he knew that these moments were fleeting. The friendships were about to change, or vanish altogether. [...] For him and Hugh, it was probably their last beer together."
(Part 1, Chapter 13, Page 108)

These words depict Keith's emotions after he learns that his father, Jesse, will run for DA. They foreshadow the coming rift between Hugh and Keith, who each remain loyal to their respective fathers as the DA Jesse takes on the crime boss Lance.

7. "'There's nothing clean about politics around here, Jesse. You're being naive. It's a dirty game.'

'It doesn't have to be.'"
(Part 2, Chapter 14, Page 114)

This exchange takes place between Rex Dubisson and Jesse when Jesse plans to run for DA the first time. Jesse's insistence that "it doesn't have to be [a dirty game]" is ironic, as he later resorts to ethically questionable tactics to achieve his goals (e.g., media smear campaigns and extortion).

8. "For Lance, it was the first sign of open warfare from Jesse Rudy."
(Part 2, Chapter 15, Page 123)

This shift in Lance's attitude occurs after Jesse, as DA, goes after Ginger and her clubs. The choice of the word "warfare," which implies death and killing, is telling, speaking to the impending violence (including Jesse's murder).

9. "Career gangsters like Lance Malco went to prison, or took a bullet, or they died in prison. That was Hugh's future too."
(Part 2, Chapter 20, Page 170)

These words foreshadow Hugh's future—dying in prison. However, the author is careful not to directly reveal Hugh's fate. Other options still exist here, like taking a bullet. By leaving Hugh's fate open, the book maintains mystery and narrative tension.

10. "Vice was perhaps the first industry to fully recover after the storm."
(Part 2, Chapter 21, Page 175)

These words refer to the recovery along the Coast following Hurricane Camille. They speak to the old adage that "nice guys finish last," as it's the everyday citizens of Biloxi who recover last after the storm—and the criminals who recover first.

11. "Nuisance law [which] allowed any citizen to file suit to enjoin another citizen from pursuing activities that were illegal and detrimental to the public good."
(Part 2, Chapter 24, Page 203)

Here, the book explains the legal basis on which Jesse arrests Ginger and, later, Lance. This is one example of how the book's author, a lawyer, takes time to explain legal terms and concepts to enhance the narrative.

12. "It was time to discuss what to do about Jesse Rudy."
(Part 2, Chapter 25, Page 215)

After Jesse targets Ginger, Lance meets with Fats to "discuss what to do about Jesse Rudy." This clearly signals that the aforementioned "war" has escalated and people plan to take direct action against Jesse.

13. "Joe Nunzio got $2,000 cash to vote not guilty."
(Part 2, Chapter 27, Page 231)

This is what's written in the anonymous note that Jesse gets during Ginger's trial. It exemplifies the deeply corrupt nature of Biloxi and introduces the concept of jury tampering, which is relevant to both Ginger's and, later, Lance's trials.

14. "Go see Cyrus Knapp, the heart doctor. He's a quack but he'll do what I say. Tell him since you got arrested you've been having chest pains, dizziness, fatigue."
(Part 2, Chapters 28-34, Page 268)

This quote is yet another example of how corrupt the criminal justice system is. These words are spoken by Lance's lawyer, who knows that he can help delay Lance's trial—and keep him out of jail longer—with these kinds of tricks.

15. "This is ruthless [...] It's blackmail."
(Part 3, Chapter 35, Page 285)

Lance's lawyer says these words to Jesse after he threatens to rat out Hugh to the FBI unless Lance takes a plea deal that includes prison time. These words epitomize the moment when Jesse, the narrative's "good guy," turns "bad," using immoral and illegal tactics to further his goals.

16. "As [Keith] and [his childhood friend] Joey left [Egan's] room and headed for the elevators, they passed Room 301, semi-private. Lying in the first bed, with his leg in the air, was the man who killed Jesse Rudy."
(Part 3, Chapter 39, Page 314)

This quote exemplifies the power of having a third-person omniscient narrator. Keith and Joey aren't aware that Jesse's killer is steps away. However, the omniscient narrator reveals how close they are to him. This allows for greater tension and excitement.

17. "Jesse Rudy's death was never mentioned. Lance had not been involved in it, and he was worried that his unpredictable son had done something stupid."
(Part 3, Chapter 43, Page 339)

Lance's view regarding Hugh's actions speaks to the dangers of being loyal—even to family. Lance isn't impressed by Hugh's loyalty but rather finds it "stupid" that Hugh tried to avenge his father.

18. "When she heard the wonderful news that she would be a grandmother, she finally broke down. The emotion was contagious, and in an instant the entire family was having a good cry. Tears of joy."
(Part 3, Chapter 44, Page 346)

This quote depicts Agnes's reaction at learning that Keith and Ainsley are having a baby. This is one of many "family moments" that the author is careful to include, emphasizing that this isn't just a crime book or a legal thriller but a tale about family.

19. "The two had once been the same size. In their glory days as twelve-year-old stars they were roughly the same height and weight, though no one bothered to measure back then. As they grew, their genes took charge."
(Part 3, Chapter 47, Page 369)

This passage occurs when Hugh and Keith appear in the courtroom simultaneously, drawing a contrast between their present and their future. The idea that "their genes took charge" directly relates to how the boys grew up to be physically different. Additionally, the mention of genetics relates to the boys' disparate familial backgrounds—the DA's son versus the crime boss' son—that guide each boy's future.

20. "Death row is the safest place in prison. There's no contact with other inmates."
(Part 4, Chapter 51, Page 405)

The final part of the book looks more closely at the US prison system and capital punishment. The idea that death row is the safest place in prison is potentially jarring—a reminder that, although imprisonment is prevalent in the book, it's a serious issue.

21. "Far from a swift and painless death, the execution was botched and it was clear that Gray suffered greatly."
(Part 4, Chapter 54, Page 420)

This description of an execution helps tease out the book's debate regarding capital punishment. The narrative doesn't offer a clear stance on whether capital punishment is right or wrong but portrays both sides of the coin through Gray's case: Gray committed an egregious act—the rape and murder of a three-year-old—and even admitted to more rapes (so he's unquestionably guilty). However, his death is so painful and grotesque that it casts doubt on whether capital punishment is ever appropriate—even for such a serious criminal.

22. "He was sixty-two years old. [...] His favorite son was on death row. His marriage was long gone. Though he still had plenty of assets, his empire was in serious decline. His friends had deserted him. [...] The Malco name, once feared and respected by man, was mud."
(Part 4, Chapter 56, Pages 435 - 436)

This quote, about Lance, illuminates another angle about the US criminal justice system that the book touches on lightly—the question of rehabilitation. Lance is one of many prisoners who struggle to find their place in the world after incarceration.

23. "I want him [Hugh] executed."
(Part 4, Chapter 58, Page 445)

*Keith says these words to the governor when the asked for his opinion regarding potential clemency for Hugh. They exemplify Keith's ruthless nature—also evident in his aggressive ascent to power (a young DA, then the youngest AG in the state, and likely a future governor). They also speak to loyalty and the theme of **Familial Identity and Legacy**, given that Keith's main aim is to avenge Jesse's death.*

24. "For a long time, I've dreamed of watching your execution, but I can't do it. I'm flying to Biloxi to sit with my mother."
(Part 4, Chapter 59, Page 454)

Keith says these words to Hugh in their final conversation, on the night of Hugh's execution. Again, these words raise questions about whether capital punishment is ever okay. Although Keith wants Hugh to die, in theory, he doesn't have the guts to watch it happen.

25. "So long, pal. I'll see you on the other side."

(Part 4, Chapter 59, Page 454)

These are the book's final words—and Hugh's final words to Keith. They epitomize the heartbreaking trajectory of "the boys" of Biloxi," Keith and Hugh: Once friends, they turn enemies, and then, at the very end, in a way friends again.

Essay Topics

1. *The Boys from Biloxi* contains four parts: "The Boys," "The Crusader," "The Prisoners," and "The Row." Consider the thematic implications of each part, relating it to that part's title. Potential topics include family identity, loyalty, morality versus legality, and legacy.

2. Baseball is a prevalent symbol throughout the book. Trace how the symbol is treated throughout the narrative and explain the significance of having baseball be the activity that binds Hugh and Keith.

3. Keith and Hugh are both extremely loyal to their fathers. However, their loyalty sometimes backfires—the best example being when Hugh wants to "avenge" Lance by ordering a hit on Jesse, and then ends up on death row. Examine the treatment of familial loyalty and how the narrative questions it.

4. Sheriff "Fats exemplifies how deeply ingrained corruption can be in a society. Trace Fats's role in supporting the book's thematic treatment of corruption, considering his trajectory throughout the narrative—from publicly dining with a crime boss to killing himself to avoid prison.

5. The media, especially the *Gulf Coast Register*, is present throughout the novel, reporting on incidents like Lance's trial and Jesse's murder. In addition, the media plays a role in politics, such as in Jesse's DA race and, later, in Keith's running for AG. What argument is the book making about the media and its relationship to politics, power, and the criminal justice system?

6. The book includes frequent descriptions of legal processes, such as jury selection and the appeals process. How does the author, a former lawyer, ensure that readers—who may not be lawyers—can follow the

details of these actions? Consider Ginger's legal case as an example. Also, consider what devices the author uses, such as including mention of real-world Supreme Court cases and using dialogue between characters.

7. Following Jesse's death, Keith becomes increasingly well-connected and ruthless in his career, climbing from DA to AG, using personal connections to the governor of Mississippi. The narrative suggests that Keith himself will one day run for governor. Discuss Keith's career aspirations and trajectory, considering the book's suggestion that corruption is apparent everywhere—including politics.

8. The final part of the book, "The Row," raises the topic of capital punishment—a notoriously touchy topic. Analyze the book's presentation of capital punishment, considering points like the narrative's inclusion of historical details (i.e., Supreme Court cases) and the case of Jimmy Lee Gray.

9. The focus of the book's action is the battle of "good versus evil," the crime fighters versus the criminals. However, even the "good guys" display morally questionable behavior, as exemplified by Jesse's resorting to extortion to lock Lance away. What argument is the book making about morality and legality?

10. The narrative focuses primarily on the opposition between criminals and the people who prosecute crime. However, the author regularly includes snippets of the Malco and Rudy families' everyday lives— graduations, weddings, births, etc. Why might the author include these details, even though they're not relevant to the main plot?

Made in United States
North Haven, CT
18 February 2023